THE STARTER KITCHEN

THE STARTER KITCHEN

Learn how to *LOVE* to cook

Callum Hann

MURDOCH BOOKS

CONTENTS

INTRODUCTION

Everyone needs to eat three meals a day for the rest of their life. This is more or less how I got interested in cooking in the first place; I have always been a huge fan of eating. This might sound ridiculous, but I think I am addicted to food. Ask anyone who knows me — I'll be planning dinner first thing in the morning, and thinking about tomorrow's breakfast as soon as that dinner is finished. I believe everyone should learn not just how to cook, but learn how to love to cook. In fact, I think you already might. If you think you don't, maybe you do and just haven't realised it yet. Cooking is truly one of the most valuable skills you can have. Let's assume you are twenty-one, like I am, and live to the ripe age of eighty-two. Assuming you do eat three meals a day, and you don't learn to cook, that's 66,795 bad experiences you'll have by then. (Yes, I was a bit of a nerd at uni.)

Up until last year I was a student living in a share house. I'm currently halfway through a mechanical engineering/sports science degree, but I decided that deferring uni to have a go on the reality television show *MasterChef* sounded like more fun — as it turned out I was fortunate enough to spend eight months doing that. I now get to do what I love every day (which I was still doing before *MasterChef*, just with exams and pub crawls in between!).

I think it was somewhat inevitable I would end up doing something with food. I grew up in the Barossa Valley in South Australia, a region famous for its food and wine. My dad worked in a winery for 27 years and my mum owns two kitchen homeware stores. My sister, Kirsty, works in a food lab and her partner, Daniel, is a chef. This brings me to the two major foodie influences of my life, my dad and Daniel.

Dad taught me the basics and how to be creative with food. He passed away from cancer in 2006, and my best memories of him revolve around food. One of my favourites is when he brought home a pasta machine. He made too much and had fettuccine drying all over the house — on the washing line, over the backs of chairs ... you get the idea.

The second major influence is Daniel. We have known each other for years, and he has always been like an older brother to me. He taught me all sorts of cooking techniques and lent me about half his bookshelf of cookbooks. He also got me a job as a kitchenhand, where I learnt how to shell prawns faster than the human eye can detect.

Most of us learn to first cook the dishes we grew up eating, and this was certainly true for me. Kirsty has been a vegetarian for most of her life, so I grew up with a significantly more vegetarian diet than most households. There's not much room to be a fussy eater as a child when your diet consists largely of vegetables!

The first experience of spreading the food bug on to others was with my two housemates, Chloe and Josh. Josh's mum had cooked him just about every meal of his life up to the point he moved in, and Chloe, her mum is an excellent cook, but she enjoys being in the kitchen about as much as she enjoys being poked in the eye. It was in our share household that I started passing my knowledge onto these guys — whether they liked it or not sometimes. I realised I loved sharing my love for food with others, and I suppose that's how this book eventually came about.

Some of the recipes in this book are the sort of food I grew up eating. Some of them I have picked up along the way from friends and colleagues. And a fair few have come about from the 'What do I have to use up in my fridge?' game we all like to play.

I think the recipes in this book will suit a whole range of budding cooks, from those who are just starting to learn the craft to those wanting to challenge themselves a bit more. I am not a writer, I am a cook, and therefore I have tried to write the recipes in the way that I would explain them to someone standing next to me, and in the way they have been explained to me at one time or another. Hopefully this makes them easy to understand.

If you remember one thing from this book, let it be: Taste what you're cooking. Not just at the end, but constantly as you are cooking. I watch a lot of people get the salt shaker and just go nuts; how do you know how much to add without tasting first? Tasting also increases your understanding of what each ingredient adds to the dish. It is this understanding that allows you to cook less to a recipe and more to your own taste. Remember, other than for baked goods, recipes are a guideline. You don't have to stress about following them to a tee. In fact, I would love you to change my recipes if it makes you like the dishes even more. If you don't like olives, don't add them! If you're a chilli freak, add ten instead of one. I want cooking for everybody to be fun and more importantly delicious.

I hope you enjoy cooking and eating the dishes in this book as much as I have and learn how to love to cook.

CALLUM HANN

BUILDING BLOCKS

After a bit of trial and error over the past few years, I have compiled some of my tips and tricks for getting the most out of my kitchen for the least effort. It includes some kitchen basics, how to choose ingredients, a list of stuff I keep in my pantry and other helpful advice to ensure cooking is fun rather than a chore.

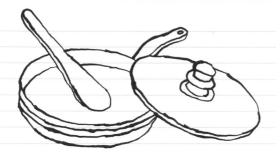

BASIC COOKING TECHNIQUES & SKILLS

To begin I thought I would just list the basic cooking methods and a quick explanation of each so if you ever come across the terms and aren't sure what they mean, you can reference them here.

FRY
This is probably the most common method of cooking. Done in a frying pan (creative name, huh?), food is cooked in a small amount of oil or butter over high heat. Try not to turn the food too often or it will tend to sweat instead of turning golden brown.

SWEAT
This is kind of the opposite to frying; it is still done in a frying pan but over a much lower heat. The food is constantly moved around so it cooks without turning golden. An example of sweating food is cooking onion for a risotto; you don't want golden brown bits of onion through your otherwise white risotto.

SHALLOW-FRY
Here food is cooked at relatively high temperatures in a frying pan with about 1.5 cm (⅝ inch) of oil. Foods that are suited to shallow-frying are those in which you want an even golden crust, but would fall apart if floating around in a deep-fryer, such as delicate fish.

DEEP-FRY

This is performed at high temperatures, generally at 140–160°C (275–315°F) to cook foods through, or at 180–190°C (350–375°F) to crisp and colour. In both instances, the food is completely submerged in hot oil. You don't need a specialty deep-fryer; I often fill my wok or a deep saucepan one-third full with oil and deep-fry on the stovetop.

STIR-FRY

Food is cooked at high temperatures in a wok. The food should be cooked quickly over high heat to retain its colour and texture. If the heat of the wok is getting away from you, and the food looks like it may burn, add a little water or stock. Don't overcrowd the wok or you will lose all the heat; cook the food in a couple of batches if you need to.

STEAM

Food is cooked in a steaming basket with a lid placed over a saucepan or wok of boiling water. A steaming basket can either be a metal container with holes in its base or a bamboo steamer with slats in its base; make sure the steaming basket doesn't touch the water below — you don't want your food sitting in water. If you use a bamboo steamer, I recommend lining the base with a small piece of baking paper or a heatproof plate to sit the food on so it doesn't stick to the bamboo (dumplings are notorious for sticking).

BOIL

Used for quickly blanching or cooking food, such as green vegetables and pasta, in a pot of rapidly boiling water.

SIMMER

When simmering, the water should still be gently bubbling away. This method is good for food that you don't want bashed around the pot too much, such as gnocchi.

POACH

A technique of cooking food very gently in water. The water should be no more than a very gentle simmer (the water should barely be moving) to allow the food to be cooked through evenly. The water can be flavoured, for example with wine, sugar or spices for poached fruit.

BRAISE

Food is submerged in liquid (usually stock, wine or water) and cooked slowly in order to make it tender and flavoursome. This technique can either be done on the stovetop on a low heat or in an oven set to a low temperature.

CONFIT

Food is submerged in oil, but unlike deep-frying confit is done at very low temperatures for a long time. This is a technique ideal for tenderising food, and it was once used as a preservation method before fridges were common.

WHISKING

Used for whipping air into light mixtures and batters, as well as incorporating mixtures to get out lumps. A balloon-shaped whisk, either hand-held or an attachment to an electric mixer, is generally the best tool.

CREAMING

Usually performed with electric beaters or an electric stand mixer and refers to beating a mixture to make it pale and creamy in consistency, such as when you beat sugar and softened butter together. Make sure the butter is really soft (not straight from the fridge) to ensure it combines with the sugar properly.

BAKE

Refers to food cooked in an oven, often in order to activate the raising agent in the food. A term used regularly in sweet and bread recipes. Baking is also used for caramelisation of sugars and to set the structure of foods such as cakes.

ROAST

Refers to food cooked in a dry oven, usually with the intention of adding flavour by making the food surface golden brown. Used predominantly for meats and vegetables.

CHOOSING INGREDIENTS

When I was studying full time, I never had bundles of cash or much time to do the grocery shopping. These are some of my favourite tips to save you time and money and still get the best ingredients.

HOW TO SHOP WELL TO SAVE MONEY

Something that really gets my goat is people who say that it's too expensive to eat well. You do have to be a little more prepared, but smart cooking (and shopping) can save you both time and money in the end. Here's my advice.

WRITE A LIST

Don't walk into a supermarket and wing it. Although it's not always practical, try to plan meals for the week ahead. It makes your shopping trip cheaper because you can buy ingredients that you will be using again later in the week in bulk. It also makes efficient use of your time; you can avoid ducking into the shops on the way home every night.

I like to split the list into three sections: fridge, fruit/veg and dry goods/miscellaneous. Having sections such as these allows you to methodically make your way around the supermarket, rather than just walking around willy-nilly.

Also, if you share food with the people you live with, it's a good idea to all go shopping together, so it is less of a chore and you can just delegate sections of the list to the other person/people.

PLAN YOUR MEAL ACCORDING TO THE SEASON

Different vegetables and fruits grow naturally at various stages throughout the year. They have different times when they are ripe and in season. Food tastes best when it is in season, there's no two ways about it. For example, tomatoes that were once only available vine-ripened in their peak during summer can now be found rosy-red 365 days of the year sitting on supermarket shelves. The artificial process involved in growing tomatoes in greenhouses, or tomatoes being brought into Australia from another country, means they never get a chance to develop a proper tomato flavour. This is why winter tomatoes tend to look great, but taste like water. In-season fruits and vegetables are also better nutritionally and are at their cheapest because they are plentiful. If you ever shop at a farmers' market, it's a great way to see what's in season because it is generally only viable for farmers to sell products that are cheap, plentiful and at their best.

GO THE EXTRA MILE

If you are shopping at a supermarket, try and buy from the deli section. It's nearly always cheaper because you don't have to pay for packaging and you reduce wastage because you can buy the exact quantity you need. Butchers and fruit and veg or farmers' markets are also great places to shop; you can usually get a better product for a cheaper price.

OTHER COST-SAVING IDEAS

- Buy ingredients that don't spoil easily in bulk.
- Try and buy the amounts you need for a recipe so you don't end up with one potato left over that you're not sure what to do with.
- When you do have left-over ingredients, try and think of ways of using them up instead of chucking them out. Most fruits can be stewed in a sugar syrup and large pots of soups are always a winner.
- Cook larger quantities than you need. Often I will cook a meal for four even if it's just for myself and one other, so that I have dinner for the following night or lunch the next day.
- Some frozen products are really good. For example, frozen peas are cheap and are pretty much as good as the real thing. Frozen berries are cheaper than fresh and you can enjoy them all year round — they're great for throwing into smoothies or cooked desserts.

CHOOSING MEAT

SHOPPING FOR MEAT

You can either buy your meat from the supermarket or from the butcher. I would recommend shopping at the butcher when you can because the meat is often of a higher standard. In addition, you are speaking to a friendly knowledgeable person about their field of expertise (note: I can't guarantee your butcher is friendly!). This means that not only do you end up buying the right cut of meat, but you can also request the exact weight you're after and aren't restricted to the shrink-wrapped packets in supermarkets. Most butchers are quite helpful as well, whether it be offering advice on cooking times or removing some pesky bones from a cut of meat.

WHAT TO LOOK FOR IN MEAT

In order for meat such as beef and lamb to develop flavour and become tender it needs to be 'hung'. If meat is bright red and wet looking, it hasn't been hung properly. Meat should be a dark red colour and rather dry looking; it shouldn't be sitting in juices or be smelly.

If the meat has thin ribbons of fat running through the flesh, it is called 'marbling'. The fat melts inside the meat and helps to keep it juicy and tender. Well-marbled meat is desirable, but it tends to be expensive. Wagyu is a well-known breed of cattle prized for its highly marbled meat.

WHICH CUT OF MEAT?

Meat can be split into two categories: primary and secondary cuts. Secondary cuts doesn't necessarily mean second best. They need to be cooked much longer than the primary cuts to make them tender, but they usually have more flavour and character. Plus they are cheap as chips.

WHAT TO LOOK FOR IN CHICKEN

The chicken should be in one piece and the skin should not be ripped or torn. The skin can vary from cream to yellow depending on the diet of the chook (corn-fed chicken will have quite yellow skin). In my personal opinion, it's worth spending a little bit extra to buy free-range or organic chickens. First, because I think they taste better. Second, I think if we are going to eat an animal, the least we can do is show it some respect by giving it a decent life. Speaking of respect, I think as a society we should try and utilise as much of the animal as possible (not just chickens, all animals!). It's good for your conscience, and it saves you money. To buy two chicken breasts will cost you almost the same as buying a whole chicken. With a whole chicken, you get the breasts, two thighs, two drumsticks, two wings and a carcass to make stock or soup from. When money was tight at uni, I would buy a chicken on Monday, and I would get enough meals out of it to last me most of the week.

CHOOSING FISH

SHOPPING FOR FISH

Fresh fish is good fish. You will get a fair idea of the quality of the fish at the supermarket or fishmongers before you even buy it. The fish should be carefully laid out, not just chucked in a pile.

WHAT TO LOOK FOR

- The fish should be moist, but not slimy.
- Fish fillets should be neatly in one piece, not falling apart.
- If the fish is whole, the eyes should look full, not sunken.
- Unpeeled shellfish should have all their legs attached.
- Lastly, smell the fish. It should smell fresh and like the sea; if it smells really strong and fishy, it has probably been sitting around for a few days.

WHICH FISH?

Fishermen rely on not only the availability of fish but also on what the weather is doing. This means that not every type of fish may be on offer at the fishmongers. Luckily, fish tends to be pretty replaceable in recipes. White fish can usually be replaced by another similarly sized white fish. Ocean trout and salmon are interchangeable. Therefore, unless a recipe insists on a certain type, choose fish that looks the best and smells the freshest on the day of buying.

FOOD SAFETY & KITCHEN HYGIENE

Food poisoning isn't much fun, but you can minimise the chance of making yourself or anyone you're cooking for sick by understanding what reduces the growth of bad bacteria in your food. Here are the factors you need to consider.

TEMPERATURE

Most bacteria can't survive beyond temperatures of around 65°C (149°F) and multiply much more slowly at temperatures less than 5°C (41°F). This leaves a prime growing temperature range from 5°C to 65°C commonly referred to as the 'danger zone' (cue dramatic music). What this means is that you need to try and minimise the time food spends in this temperature range (read about How to Store Food Without Poisoning People on pages 10–12).

FOODS

There are foods that are particularly susceptible to bacteria growth: raw meat or fish, dairy products and cooked stuff (rice, pasta and soups, for example) are excellent breeding grounds for bacteria. So make sure you cool these cooked foods down as quickly as possible, and when you buy refrigerated stuff from the supermarket make sure you get it into your fridge at home as soon as possible or invest in a cooler bag to carry goods while you're shopping; the more time it spends out of the fridge, the higher chance of bacteria growing.

TIPS FOR PREPARATION & AVOIDING CROSS-CONTAMINATION

- If you're cooking a chicken breast and turning it with tongs, then don't serve it with those tongs before cleaning them as they will still have the bacteria from the uncooked chicken on them. Always use clean tongs or spoons for serving.
- Wash a chopping board that has had raw meat, poultry or fish on it before you use it for anything else to avoid spreading bacteria onto other foods. Actually, if you have a few chopping boards, it's not bad idea to have one that you use just for meat, one just for fish and so on.
- Replace kitchen cloths regularly. You can even chuck them in the microwave from time to time; microwaving nukes the bacteria out of just about anything.
- Wipe your work surfaces down with an antibacterial kitchen cleaner regularly. It's easier to do a quick spray and wipe down after you cook rather than letting your bench load up with scummy stuff for days on end.
- Wash your hands before cooking, and again after handling raw meat, poultry or seafood, and after sneezing or going to the bathroom.
- You should only reheat food once.

HOW TO STORE FOOD WITHOUT POISONING PEOPLE

REFRIGERATING FOOD

- Keep raw meat in a container or on a plate so it doesn't drip juices onto other food. It's also a good idea to keep it on the bottom shelf of your fridge. Similarly, foods that are ready to eat, such as cheese or cooked food, should be kept on the higher shelves.

- Keep most fruit and vegetables in the crisper of your fridge. When you buy food at the supermarket, it's a dead giveaway to how it should be stored: vegetables such as onions, potatoes and garlic are kept out of the fridge at the supermarket, so keep them out of your fridge for best storage; they can be kept in a cupboard or pantry.
- Keep eggs in the fridge and take them out as you need them.
- The 'danger zone' (sounds ominous right?) is the temperature range from 5°C (41°F) to 65°C (149°F). This is when bacteria grows quickly, so food such as chicken needs to either be hot or in the fridge/freezer, so it spends as little time as possible in this temperature range. If you have leftovers, you want to cool them down as quickly as possible, so put the hot food into shallow containers to cool, then transfer to the fridge and cover with a lid. Only cover the food once it has cooled down. Don't make the common mistake of tightly wrapping the top of a bowl of hot food in plastic wrap — the steamy environment creates a solid breeding ground for bacteria. If you want to cover the food while it's hot, place the plastic wrap directly over the surface of the food, not the rim of the bowl. It's also better not to put hot food in the fridge immediately as it will warm up the other items in the fridge.
- Leftovers can generally be kept for 1–2 days in the fridge, or longer in the freezer.

FREEZING FOOD

- You can freeze most things with pretty good results. Here is a list of things that I recommend *not* freezing (as they aren't very nice once thawed):
  - Green vegetables, such as lettuce, cabbage, celery and cucumber.
  - Cooked rice and pasta.
  - Dairy items, such as cream, milk and custard (grated cheese is okay though).
  - Mayonnaise.
  - Anything fried.
- Get in the habit of thawing frozen food slowly in the refrigerator. You can thaw it quickly in the microwave on 'defrost', but that causes all sorts of problems as some parts of the food may start to cook, while others are still frozen solid.
- Liquid expands when frozen, so don't fill containers right to the top.
- Don't refreeze thawed food.

- If you want to freeze vegetables, it's a good idea to blanch them in boiling water for a couple of minutes first. This helps them keep their colour, flavour and texture.
- Make sure the food is covered and in sealed containers or freezer bags. Remove as much air as possible from freezer bags to avoid freezer burn.
- Use containers with straight sides as it makes frozen food much easier to get out.
- It's a good idea to label foods you're going to freeze with their contents and the date. When it goes in the freezer, I know it's chicken soup, but when it's a frozen brown block and I'm trying to figure out what the heck it is three months down the track, I'm thankful for that label!

IN THE PANTRY

Keep food in airtight containers, or tie a rubber band tightly around any open packets. Open food packets can let in weevils, which are not a very nice surprise the next time you go to use the flour. There's nothing worse than not knowing which container is plain (all-purpose) flour and which is self-raising. I once made that very mistake and my brownies turned into a cake, and not a great cake at that. Label containers so you know what's in them without having to hire a private investigator.

STUFF I ALWAYS HAVE IN MY PANTRY

Don't treat your pantry as a graveyard for half-used ingredients. If you kit out your pantry properly, there may be an initial cost but it means that you can often whip up a delicious meal with only a few fresh ingredients. The essentials are different for everyone, depending on what sort of food you cook most. If you don't like desserts, you can probably skip on ingredients such as icing (confectioner's) sugar and chocolate. Just remember that the use-by or best-before date only applies before the product has been opened; it will need to be used sooner once opened. The following ingredients are what I like to have in my kitchen at all times.

PANTRY

KEEP FOR UP TO 6 MONTHS

- Dried breadcrumbs.
- Spices: cumin, coriander, cinnamon, paprika, turmeric, black pepper and vanilla beans are what I can't live without. It's also handy to have mixed spices on hand, such as Indian garam masala and Chinese five-spice. Spices last longer than six months, but they will lose their flavour.

KEEP FOR UP TO 9 MONTHS

- Flours: plain (all-purpose), self-raising and cornflour (cornstarch). These are useful for baking, thickening sauces and crumbing.

KEEP FOR UP TO 12 MONTHS

- Dried pasta: keep a few different shapes and sizes.
- Rice: arborio for risotto, jasmine or basmati for Asian or Indian dishes respectively.
- Couscous.
- Polenta.
- Vinegar: white wine and balsamic.
- Olive and vegetable oils.

CHECK THE USE-BY DATE

- Nuts: hazelnuts, peanuts and walnuts are some of my favourites. Great crunch for salads or chucking into desserts.
- Tinned lentils, chickpeas and cannellini (white) beans. I love making hummus so chickpeas are a must. Plus, these pulses are great to add to soups and curries at the end of cooking to make them much more filling and hearty.
- Tinned chopped tomatoes.
- Tinned tuna — get the stuff in olive oil, not brine.
- Coconut milk.
- Sauces: soy, fish, oyster, hoisin (check if they need to be refrigerated).
- Chocolate (which makes a more than acceptable dessert if you're feeling lazy).

KEEP UNTIL FLYING CARS ARE INVENTED

- Sea salt.
- Caster (superfine) sugar has small granules that dissolve quickly, and it's ideal for making desserts, such as meringue and caramel.
- Icing (confectioner's) sugar is great for making sweet pastry and buttercream icing for cakes.

FREEZER

- Vanilla ice cream comes in very handy to have with desserts, or as a dessert on its own.
- Frozen berries are good all year round and pretty cheap compared to the fresh product.
- Frozen peas.
- Frozen shortcrust and puff pastry.

FRIDGE

- Butter.
- Milk.
- Juice.
- Cheese — I usually have cheddar and parmesan on hand.
- Eggs.
- Mustard is great in dressings and marinades, and on sandwiches.

KEEPING SOME LAW & ORDER IN YOUR PANTRY

When you're putting the shopping away, it will save you time
down the track if you put like items together logically in the pantry.
I have spices, oil, vinegar, sauces and tinned goods, such as tomatoes,
together on a shelf at eye level because I use them every day. I have
a shelf devoted to flour, sugar, pasta, rice, nuts and other dry goods
because I use these a bit less often. A bit of a shelf is home to
breakfasty stuff, including jams, honey, peanut butter and cereal.
My bottom shelf contains spare food, such as excess oil, and also
houses onions and potatoes (as they need to be kept somewhere dry,
dark and cool). On my top shelf I keep wine and spirits, though I'm
not really sure why — I think they were always on the top shelf when
I was a kid so I couldn't reach them and it's a habit I've kept. By all
means have your own (probably more logical) system, but it is way
easier if you, and the people you are with, know exactly where they
have to look when a recipe calls for paprika, say.

KITCHEN EQUIPMENT

Here's a list of what I think are the essential tools and gadgets for any kitchen.

HAND-HELD STUFF

KNIVES

I think good knives are probably the most important equipment to have. A good knife block is expensive and, in my opinon, fairly unnecessary. You often get a big knife, a bread knife, a small knife and a couple of other knives for vague purposes. When I got my first knives, I went out and bought a 30 cm (12 inch) cook's knife and a small paring knife. I still use both of these knives today, along with a few others purchased as I needed them, such as a cleaver and filleting knife. I think you're better off spending $100 on one good cook's knife than $150 on a set of knives. Your cook's knife is by far the most important. You want a knife that feels comfortable in your hand, and the weight should feel right. You also want there to be a decent distance between the bottom of the blade and the bottom of the handle. This ensures your knuckles aren't smashing into the chopping board as you work. You also need a small paring knife for peeling and trimming fruit and vegetables. A serrated knife is handy to have, but a cheap one will do.

One of the most important things you need to do in the kitchen, and this is the one job most people neglect, is sharpening your knives. It doesn't matter how good your knife is, if you don't sharpen it regularly, it will be blunt and make your job much harder. Plus, it's less safe to work with a blunt knife. Unless you're really confident with a steel, I would suggest investing in one of the new water-wheel-style sharpeners. They are foolproof to use and keep any knife super sharp.

WOODEN SPOON (OR THREE)
Must-haves for any kitchen. If you leave a plastic or metal spoon in a pan while you go to answer the phone, you'll either have a melted spoon or a burnt hand; a wooden spoon is much more forgiving. And it won't scratch non-stick pans either.

MEASURING CUPS, SPOONS AND SCALES
Unless you are one heck of an estimator, pastry and dessert measurements should be followed strictly or you'll end up with rock-hard panna cotta and sunken cakes. With savoury food, you can wing it a bit more, as long as it matches your personal taste. Australian standard measuring spoons and cups are slightly more than the US equivalents. One Australian tablespoon equals 20 ml (¾ fl oz) or 4 teaspoons and one Australian cup equals 250 ml (9 fl oz).

COLANDER AND FINE-MESH SIEVE
You will need a colander for draining pasta or cooked vegetables. A fine-mesh sieve is great for getting the lumps out of dry goods such as flour or almond meal (ground almonds). They're also pretty handy for straining sauces and purées.

GRATER OR ZESTER
Box graters are handy for grating large quantities of cheese or vegetables. Try and get one with a handle on top so you don't grate your fingers. I think it's well worth investing in a Microplane rasp zester rather than the dodgy little blunt zesters that make grating really hard work. A Microplane is great because you can grate ginger or cheese as well as zest citrus on the sharp blades.

INCIDENTALS
Tongs, balloon whisk, vegetable peeler, potato masher, big serving spoon, slotted spoon, ladle and regular metal cutlery spoons for tasting are all essentials. In fact, you should never be too far from a spoon when you are cooking.

USED ON THE STOVETOP OR IN THE OVEN

LARGE HEAVY-BASED SAUCEPAN

You want a pan with a big heavy chunk of metal (preferably 'sandwiched') on the base. This ensures the pan heats evenly and maintains that heat. (A thin pan will get hot-spots and just burn food.) This is your go-to pan for many dishes, from soups to curries to braises. You want one that is suitable for going into the oven as well as cooking on the stovetop.

NON-STICK FRYING PAN

Brilliant to cook with provided you look after it. I would recommend using tongs with silicone ends rather than metal, which will scratch your pan. Just don't leave the tongs sitting in the pan or the ends will melt. Try and get a frying pan that has a metal handle rather than plastic so it can go straight into the oven from the stovetop.

OTHER SAUCEPANS

While you should buy a decent heavy-based saucepan and non-stick frying pan, you can get away with cheapish saucepans for everyday cooking. Still try and get some that feel heavy for their size, though. One big saucepan and one or two smaller saucepans should be more than enough. These are ideal for boiling/steaming vegetables, cooking pasta or rice, and heating liquids.

WOK

This is really useful to have for making quick dinners, such as stir-fries and light curries. It can lend itself to different cooking techniques, from stir-frying and steaming to deep-frying. Round-based woks are best for gas burners (you will also need a trivet for it to sit on), but if you have an electric stove, you will need a wok with a flat base.

ROASTING TRAY AND BAKING TRAYS

Try and find a nice heavy-based roasting tray capable of going on the stovetop (i.e. metal, not ceramic or glass) and in the oven. This way you can start dishes on the stovetop and transfer them to the oven, or for roasts you can take out the meat and make the gravy in the tray.

USED ON THE BENCH

CHOPPING BOARDS

You can find chopping boards made from different materials: wood, plastic and even glass. If you buy a glass chopping board, I will personally hunt you down, though. They are terrible for your knife and slip easily, making them dangerous. Get a nice big sturdy chopping board, so it's not slipping around when you're trying to cut on it. It is also less likely to warp and change shape over time. Wooden boards shouldn't be completely submerged in water or they might crack. Rub them with oil from time to time to make sure they last. I like to use a separate plastic board for meat and fish as they are the most hygienic.

FOOD PROCESSOR

Fantastic for making curry pastes and other flavour bases, coarsely chopping ingredients or bringing together doughs.

BLENDER

Handy for making smoothies or liquidising soups.

BOWLS

Get a set of bowls, preferably heatproof and non-reactive, that sit inside each other for easy storage, like a fine set of babushka dolls. I prefer metal bowls because they are lightweight and you can bash them around a fair bit without having to worry about them breaking. Just make sure if you put hot liquids in them, you use a dry tea towel or oven mitts to move them around as the metal conducts heat very well and the rim of the bowl can get scalding hot. Glass bowls give you a good result but they can be a little clunky. I would avoid plastic bowls as they can be a hassle to clean and can retain flavours.

AND IF YOU LIKE DESSERT

CAKE TINS
Look for tins with a non-stick surface to reduce the chances of your cake sticking. Although, it's still a good idea to grease and line even non-stick tins with baking paper to be certain.

PIPING BAG/NOZZLES
Useful for piping icing onto cakes, shaping little biscuits or macarons, piping fillings, making meringues or choux pastry into the desired shapes, and serving mousse. Personally, I hate washing piping bags, so I'm a fan of the disposable kind. You can even use zip-lock bags with the corner snipped off as long as you have nozzles. Get a set of nozzles of different sizes, ranging from 2 mm (1/16 inch) to about 15 mm (5/8 inch).

INCIDENTALS
It's well worth getting a good-quality flexible spatula, and possibly even a sugar thermometer and oven thermometer if you like making desserts as much as I do.

SAFETY IN THE KITCHEN

I don't want to lecture you too much about safety, so feel free to skip over this stuff if you're a seasoned cook. If you're newer to the kitchen, I think it's worth having a squiz at this section. As much as kitchens are fun places, all the sharp objects and hot things can be dangerous if not treated carefully.

NO-KIDS ZONE

Kitchens are naturally a somewhat hazardous place in the house. So don't let young children wander around you while you are cooking. The same goes for pets; you would hate to trip over your dog while carrying a saucepan full of boiling water. For similar reasons, don't have sharp objects near the edge of the bench, and make sure that pan handles face inward or to the side of the stovetop, and are not hanging over the edge.

BURNS

If you ever burn yourself in the kitchen, hold the burn under cold running water for 20 minutes. Don't do anything else. I have seen people use ice, gels and toothpaste to apparently 'cure' burns among other things.

If you are making caramel or sugar syrups, it's a good idea to have a bowl of cold water nearby to dip a burn into if necessary. If you do get hot sugar on you, don't try and peel it off straight away or you will pull off your skin with it; get it straight into cold water.

COMMUNICATION

I love having cooking sessions with mates, so to make sure it stays fun be courteous to each other. In a commercial kitchen, whenever chefs walk behind each other they say 'behind!', 'backs!' or similar. You don't want to suddenly swing around with a knife and give your friend an unwanted haircut.

CLOTHING

I'm all for keeping it casual in the kitchen, but it's a good idea to wear shoes. I know a guy who was cooking in bare feet, knocked his knife off the bench and managed to sever a tendon in his foot. Needless to say he was on crutches for a while. It's also a good idea to tie back your hair if it's long, and wear an apron, particularly if you are deep-frying.

TEA TOWELS ARE YOUR FRIEND

It sounds obvious, but always pick up anything evenly remotely hot with a dry tea towel or oven mitts (wet ones will conduct heat more quickly). I keep a tea towel on me at all times when I'm busy in the kitchen so I'm never searching for something to use.

AVOID HUGE PILES OF DISHES

I like to fill a sink full of hot soapy water as I start cooking, so that when I have a spare minute (for example, waiting for a pot of water to boil) I can quickly wash a few dishes. This helps to avoid the precarious stacks of dishes that are no fun to wash at the end. When I do have a big stack, I like to put on my iPod and the time always goes pretty quickly.

HOW TO USE A KNIFE SAFELY
{AND LOOK IMPRESSIVE}

Read the tips below and try and put them into practice.
You'll look like a pro in no time.

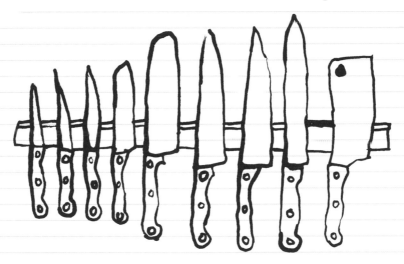

SECURING YOUR CHOPPING BOARD

There are two common ways people cut themselves: the knife
slipping or the board slipping. So if we can remove the chance of
the board slipping, we're halfway to avoiding a knife injury. The
best chopping boards are heavy and thick, so they don't warp and
rock around as you cut (see page 19). Benches and chopping boards
are both smooth surfaces, so boards tend to slide around a bit.
If you dampen a cloth or a couple of pieces of paper towel and place
the board on these, you can increase the friction between the board
and the bench, and therefore make your board much more steady.
It will take you 10 seconds to do this and it will make your chopping
experience a far more pleasant one.

KEEP YOUR BOARD CLEAN

I like to have a little bowl or disposable bag on my bench next to my board at all times. When I have any food scraps: garlic skin, pumpkin seeds (pepitas), apple cores, I put these straight into the bowl or bag. Once you are done prepping, you can just empty the bag into the bin. This means when you go to dice your onion, you don't have to squeeze yourself onto a corner of the board and work around all the crap taking over your workspace. Actually, cleaning your general workspace as you go, too, saves you time in the long run. I like to keep a damp cloth on my bench and wipe down the surface every time I start a new job. It makes cleaning up at the end ten times easier.

SLICE, DON'T CHOP

A knife is more effective at cutting when it is slicing food, not pushing down on it. This allows the knife to do the work, rather than having to force it. The best way to slice food is to use a rocking motion, where you start with the tip of the knife touching the board with the handle raised, then slide it down and forward until the heel of the knife is touching the board. You then rock back to the tip, with the knife in contact with the board the whole time. This way you are getting clean cuts by using the length of the knife. Secondly, you are less likely to cut yourself because there is some part of the knife touching the board at all times. Cutting food should almost be silent, rather than violent thuds made by forcing the knife down.

CRAB CLAW & VERTICAL FINGERS

If you're right handed, there are two main positions you'll need for your left hand (vice-versa for lefties). The first is what I like to call the crab claw, and is used for cutting foods that don't have a flat surface, such as cutting an onion in half. Hold the food firmly with your thumb and four fingers on opposite sides of the food. Carefully slice the food with the blade of the knife between your thumb and fingers.

The second is for slicing herbs, dicing vegetables and most general knife use. You want the middle part of your fingers perpendicular to the board and your fingertips and thumb curled underneath, then rest the flat side of a knife against your vertical fingers. It seems to go against intuition to have your fingers touching the blade, but this allows you to guide the knife (so it won't slip) without getting your fingertips in the way. This is much safer than having your fingers flat on the board because if your knife slips, you're in big trouble.

EYES ON THE PRIZE

Your eyes should be directly over the top of your knife. This helps you to see where the blade is in relation to your fingers and helps you to get nice straight, consistent cuts. If your eyes are to the left or right of the blade, you'll tend to end up cutting on an angle instead of perpendicular to the board.

SHARPEN YOUR KNIFE

A sharp knife is a safe knife, as you don't need to force it through food when cutting. It will easily glide through instead. Steels (long metal rods that butchers have hanging off their belts) can be difficult to use correctly. I think one of the best ways to keep your knives sharp is to use a ceramic wheel to run your knife back and forth on. Try and sharpen your knives a little every few times you use them, rather than letting them become super blunt.

KEEP YOUR KNIFE CLEAN

Lastly, wash your knife in some hot soapy water, dry it well and put it away immediately. I have a nice little scar on my hand from when a food processor blade was left in the bottom of a full sink. I plunged my hand into the sink (not knowing the sharp fate that awaited me) and ended up with three stitches. It could have been a lot worse.

COOKING WITHOUT A RECIPE

If you are not particularly confident in the kitchen, then by all means follow the recipes in this book to a tee. As you become more confident with specific recipes or cooking in general, you will probably start ditching the recipe and cook more instinctively. I certainly encourage this — it is how I love to cook, adding a 'splash' of wine or a 'glug' of oil. Just note that with baking or dessert recipes it's a good idea to follow the main part of the recipe to ensure it turns out properly (but it doesn't mean you can't change what you serve with it).

If you start making up your own recipes, here are a few loose guidelines you can follow in order to make sure you're happy with the end result.

TASTE

Whenever you are cooking, taste the food constantly. The four tastes your tongue can detect are sweet, sour, salty and bitter (and there is a fifth taste, umami, but let's not get into that now) and generally you want to create a harmony between these. It's not necessarily adding sugar or salt to a dish, as these tastes come in many shapes and sizes. The sweetness in your dish may come from slowly cooked onions, which become sweet and jammy; the sour may come from balsamic vinegar; and the saltiness may come from some shaved parmesan. Similarly, meat cooked in a rich, sticky sauce may benefit from being served with some green vegetables, which have a natural bitterness.

So, if you have made something and it tastes nice but you think it could be improved, think of an ingredient you could add to balance the flavours. Remember, it's always best to add a little bit at first; you can always add more soy sauce but it's pretty hard to take it out.

TEXTURE

This is the part of food that doesn't get enough credit, and in many ways it is as important as flavour. Just as much as you try to balance flavours, textures should be balanced, from soft, crunchy and crispy to ... You get the idea. How much better is a silky smooth soup with a thick slice of crusty bread? Do you love hot chips because (a) you can't get enough of that great potato taste or (b) they are crisp on the outside and soft and fluffy on the inside? The answer I'm looking for here is (b) and I would also accept an answer of (c): because they are packed with salty deliciousness.

Think of ways to bring an extra texture to the food you cook. Texture is so important in making every bite of food you eat slightly different so that it doesn't become boring. There are two ways of doing this: either by adding a new ingredient (such as almonds for crunch or feta cheese for smoothness) or changing the texture of an existing ingredient, such as deep-frying tofu so it is both crisp and soft.

PLANNING A MENU

The above points about taste and texture apply to individual dishes, but they also apply to meals as a whole. Let's say a pasta dish may be served in a rich, sweet tomato sauce with parmesan on top. Delicious on its own, but serve it with a peppery rocket (arugula) salad with walnuts and a dressing and you are balancing the meal as a whole, so that the meal becomes more than just the sum of its parts. Are you catching what I'm throwing? I hope you use some of the recipes in this book together to form grand meals for certain occasions. You can read some of my recommendations in Menu Ideas (see pages 173–179).

COOKING & SHARING FOOD WITH OTHERS

I thought I would chip in my opinion on sharing food with the people you live with. Typically there are two ways in which the food situation operates in your house and I'm sure you can relate to one of these: (a) all the food is shared and the costs too, or (b) everything is separate, everyone has their own shelf in the pantry and there are about three loaves of bread kicking around at any one time.

I understand the rationale of option (b) if you are perhaps living with people who you have only just met, but I think in most situations shared food is the way to go, and here are just a few reasons why.

COST

You can really take advantage of buying in bulk when you share food. Rather than spending $6 on a tiny little container of coffee, spend $10 with a couple of people for a much larger one and it will last much longer.

MAKES SHOPPING EASIER

Shopping by yourself is a chore, not much fun at all. If you go with the people you live with, not only is it much more fun, but it is also really quick too. I used to have a little tin that we would all put $50 in each week. We would then use this 'kitty' for buying the groceries, as well as stuff such as paper towel and dish-washing liquid. Left-over money was used for a coffee at the end of the shopping trip or beers for Friday night.

COOKING IS A GOOD WAY TO SPEND TIME WITH THE PEOPLE YOU LIVE WITH

Everyone has to eat, so you may as well enjoy your time in the kitchen. I think it's a great social activity. Put the radio on, have a chat and share a beer with your housemate/s. It's also a great way to cook new things because chances are the dishes they like to cook are different from yours.

LESS WASTED SPACE

Your fridge will have way more room for beer if you don't have duplicates of everything.

REDUCES FOOD WASTAGE

I think that when everyone has individual food, it's much harder to get through it by the use-by date. If you buy a 2 litre (70 fl oz) bottle of milk to share, the use-by date is almost meaningless as it's all consumed within days; 2 litres alone and you find yourself drinking four glasses of milk the day after it is out of date!

KITCHEN KNOW HOW

People always have an excuse as to why they can't or won't cook. Cooking doesn't have to be difficult, expensive or a chore. Some of my best friends couldn't cook, which was a bit of an issue when they moved away from home. Honestly, for about a year they lived off takeaway/two-minute noodles/deep-frying anything from a frozen packet. I decided I wanted to teach them. I promise you, if they can learn to cook, anyone can!

This chapter is all about the foundations of cooking. This was some of the first stuff I learnt in the kitchen, and these basics often use the most humble and affordable ingredients, so it's well worth taking the time to practise them.

When you are cooking a recipe, I recommend you first read it completely from start to finish, so you understand everything you will have to do before beginning.

MY RICE TIPS

Rice is a great ingredient to have in your pantry because it's cheap as chips and its subtle taste complements heaps of dishes.

CHOOSING YOUR RICE

Different types of rice lend themselves better to certain dishes. Below are the main types I use. Allow ⅓–½ cup raw rice per person.

RICE VARIETY	CHARACTERISTICS	SUITABLE USES
jasmine	high starch	Thai/Malaysian curries
	sticks together, so suitable	Chinese dishes
	for chopsticks	Japanese dishes
basmati	low starch	Indian dishes
	grains remain separate	
arborio	high starch	risotto
	creamy result	rice desserts
short-grain	medium starch	sushi
	just sticks together	rice desserts

BEFORE COOKING

If you want the rice grains to stay separate after cooking, it's a good idea to wash the rice in a sieve before cooking. This gets rid of any excess starch. This is worth doing for basmati rice, but not for arborio because you want the starch to make a creamy risotto.

COOKING

There are a couple of ways you can cook rice, but I think the best approach is the absorption method. The idea is to use just enough liquid so that the rice will absorb it all during the cooking time and not require draining. The rule of thumb for two or less cups of rice is a ratio of 1 part rice to 1.5 parts liquid. The liquid does not necessarily have to be water; you can replace some or all of the water with stock or coconut milk. Combine the rice and water in a saucepan with a tight-fitting lid, bring to the boil, reduce the heat to low and cook for 12 minutes. Remove from the heat and leave for 10 minutes with the lid on, then serve.

MY PASTA TIPS

Cooking pasta is pretty straightforward. Below is a general guide not just for this book, but for all your favourite pasta recipes.

CHOOSING YOUR PASTA

Before you decide what pasta to use, you need to decide what sauce you are serving with it. Pasta can be broken up into the following categories.

PASTA TYPE	EXAMPLES	SUITABLE SAUCES OR USES
filled	ravioli, tortellini	tomato-based
		thicker sauces such as pesto
short	fusilli, orecchiette	chunky vegetable
		soups
		broths
tube	penne, macaroni	tomato-based
		cheese-based
		meat sauces
		pasta bakes
long and thin	spaghetti, linguine	oil-based
		seafood
long and wide	fettuccine, pappardelle	creamy sauces
		butter sauces
		meat sauces
		tomato-based

BEFORE COOKING

Fill your biggest pot two-thirds full with water. Add a generous amount of salt and bring to a rolling boil. Use more salt than you think necessary; it helps to season the pasta as it's cooking and most of it will be left in the water anyway. If your pasta is well seasoned before it goes into the sauce, you will need to add less salt to your finished dish.

Some people add oil to the cooking water to stop the pasta sticking. It is not necessary; as long as you stir occasionally and the water is boiling for the duration of the cooking time the pasta won't stick.

COOKING

As a general rule, allow 100 g (3½ oz) dried pasta per person. Once your water is boiling like crazy, add your pasta, stir and put a lid on until the water returns to the boil. Remove the lid, and boil until 'al dente' which translates as 'to the tooth'. This is basically the point where the pasta is just cooked but not so soft that it's like eating mush. Once you're happy with how it is cooked scoop out a glass of salty cooking water to use in the sauce if you like.

AFTER COOKING

Drain the pasta in a colander in the sink, shaking it around to get rid of any excess water. Toss it straight into your hot pasta sauce. If the sauce is really thick and needs loosening up, use some of the salty hot water you, hopefully, kept from earlier. Eat your pasta straight away.

HOW TO COOK THE PERFECT STEAK

I love a good steak on the barbecue with a salad in summer, or maybe cooked in a pan in winter with some mashed potato or chips. I think if you're going to pay good money for a piece of beef, you may as well make it taste amazing, so here are some tips to get it bang-on.

BEFORE COOKING

Take the meat out of the fridge an hour before you start cooking as room-temperature meat cooks more evenly.

Cut any excess sinew off the meat as the sinew loosens the meat and stops it from tightening up and shrinking when it cooks.

Oil the meat, not the pan. This reduces the chance of the oil burning and flames on an open barbecue. Sure, it looks impressive, but burnt oil or burnt meat doesn't taste good enough to justify the heroics.

Season the meat just before you cook it. Don't be too stingy with the salt as it helps form a delicious golden brown crust on the outside of the meat. Seasoning before cooking helps the steak absorb the salt; if you add salt afterwards most of it will fall off.

COOKING

One of the most important things is to make sure you have a screaming hot pan to begin with. If the meat doesn't give a decent sizzle when you first lay it in the pan, then it's not hot enough — and you won't get a beautiful golden brown layer on the meat. Don't be that person who serves grey steaks because you started with a cold pan.

Don't play with the meat. You only want to turn the steak over once.

Everyone likes his or her steak cooked differently, so once all the steaks are on ask your guests what their preferences are. This makes you look chivalrous and like you know what you're doing.

AFTER COOKING

It's important to rest the meat after cooking before you cut into it. Resting allows the meat to relax and retain its juices inside. A rare steak shouldn't bleed all over the plate if rested properly. The rule of thumb is to rest the steak for half the time that it was cooked. You obviously don't want the meat to go cold, so the best way is to transfer the cooked steak to a hot plate and cover it with a clean tea towel.

I haven't included cooking times in the table because they depend on the cut of meat used and its thickness, and how hot your pan or grill is to start.

You can also feel how cooked meat is by pressing it in the middle with your finger or a pair of tongs. When meat is rare, it will be really soft and squishy, and gets firmer the longer you cook it. Lots of people say that if you pinch your thumb and index finger together, the meaty part of your palm under your thumb feels like a medium–rare steak, middle finger and thumb is medium, ring finger and thumb is medium–well and pinkie and thumb represents well done. I'm a bit sceptical, because everyone has different hands, but it's not a bad guide.

When cutting meat, you want to cut across the grain (whether it's cooked or raw) to make it as tender as possible.

A BIT ABOUT EGGS

Here are a few of my favourite methods of cooking the humble egg. If you aren't in the habit already, I recommend buying free-range eggs. Hopefully you will notice they taste better and, even if you don't, you can feel better about yourself from an ethical point of view.

The most important thing to remember when making scrambled eggs is that they continue to cook after you take them out of the pan. You need to take them off the heat while they still look a bit undercooked or you will end up with really dry eggs. I like to eat them with crispy bacon and some roasted cherry tomatoes or mushrooms.

SCRAMBLED EGGS

PREPARATION TIME 5 MINUTES // COOKING TIME 5 MINUTES // SERVES 2

5 eggs
60 ml (2 fl oz/¼ cup) pouring (single) cream
1 tablespoon finely chopped chives (optional)
30 g (1 oz) butter
toast, to serve

1. Place the eggs, cream and chives in a bowl and whisk until just combined. Don't stress if there are a few little lumps of egg yolk.

2. Heat a small frying pan over low heat, add the butter and, once it has melted and foamed a bit, add the egg mixture. Use a flat-ended wooden spoon or heatproof rubber spatula to occasionally push the edges in towards the centre, letting the uncooked egg flow towards the edges. If you cook the eggs nice and slowly, folding occasionally with the spoon, you'll get a beautiful creamy consistency. When the eggs are slightly undercooked, about 2–4 minutes, season to taste with salt and remove from the heat. Spoon onto the toast and serve.

I never used to ask for poached eggs because I thought the fact they were just cooked in water would mean they would be bland and tasteless. I have now grown to love them — with some charred asparagus and smoked salmon, perhaps, or maybe with some mashed avocado on toast. Recipes often tell you to make a whirlpool in the water before adding the eggs. I've tried it both ways, and haven't found that it gives a better result. The most important thing I've found is that the eggs need to be really fresh — the white should cling firmly to the yolk. With an older egg, the white is really runny and will go everywhere in the pot when you tip it in. A good way to tell the freshness of an egg is to place it in water; a really fresh one will be heavy and sink to the bottom and lay flat, while the tip of a less fresh one will start to float, and for a really old one the whole egg will float.

POACHED EGGS

PREPARATION TIME 5 MINUTES // COOKING TIME 3 MINUTES // SERVES 2

4 really fresh large eggs
toast, to serve

1. Get a large saucepan and half fill it with hot water. Add a big pinch of salt, then bring to a really gentle simmer over medium heat.
2. Crack an egg into a cup or small bowl. Get the cup or bowl near the surface of the water, then slip the egg into the saucepan. Repeat with the remaining eggs. Cook for 3 minutes or until the whites are firm but not hard.
3. Remove the eggs with a slotted spoon, letting any excess water drain off, then place on paper towel to absorb any excess water. Season to taste with salt and pepper and serve immediately on toast.

This makes for a really satisfying breakfast or even dinner if you make a salad to go with it. I often double or triple the quantity of the chorizo sauce and keep it in my fridge. That way, when I wake up after a few beers from the night before, all I have to do is crack a couple of eggs and a delicious breakfast isn't far away.

CHORIZO BAKED EGGS

PREPARATION TIME 15 MINUTES // COOKING TIME 35 MINUTES // SERVES 4

1. Preheat the oven to 200°C (400°F/Gas 6).
2. Heat the oil in a deep frying pan over medium–high heat, add the chorizo and cook for 4 minutes or until golden, then add the onion and capsicum and cook, stirring occasionally, for 4 minutes or until the onion is translucent. Add the garlic and paprika and cook for a further minute. Add the tomatoes, reduce the heat to medium and simmer for 15 minutes or until thickened. Season to taste with salt and pepper.
3. Divide the mixture among four 300 ml (10½ fl oz) capacity ramekins. Crack an egg over each and top with the cheese. Bake for 8–10 minutes or until the eggs are just set.
4. Top with a little parsley and serve with the toasted ciabatta.

1 tablespoon olive oil
1 fresh chorizo sausage, thinly sliced
1 red onion, thinly sliced
1 red capsicum (pepper), seeds removed and diced
3 garlic cloves, thinly sliced
2 teaspoons hot paprika
2 x 400g (14 oz) tins chopped tomatoes
4 eggs
65 g (2⅓ oz/⅔ cup) coarsely grated cheddar cheese
2 tablespoons chopped flat-leaf (Italian) parsley, to serve
toasted ciabatta, to serve

RECIPES

The following chapters are my pride and joy. They contain the recipes that I have made for late-night dinners, quick lunches, special occasions and the odd hangover. I have made them over and over, but I don't think they ever turn out exactly the same, and I don't expect them to. If you don't have or like an ingredient, substitute it for something similar. There are no right or wrong answers with food, as long as you think it tastes good! Hopefully you use the recipes as a guide, and change them over time until they become your own. With any luck you'll have as much fun making them as I have!

THE QUICK AND THE FED

A lot of people tell me they don't cook because they don't have enough time, so here are some of my go-to recipes when I want something quick but despite the short cooking time doesn't compromise on flavour. The first time you cook a dish it will be the most expensive because you have to buy the fresh produce as well as the pantry goods. Usually once you have these pantry items they will last you a while and the total cost of the dish will work out to be cheaper than takeaway meals.

None of the recipes in this chapter should take you more than 25 minutes from opening the fridge to dinner on the table. I've included a couple of super-quick desserts too because even when you are struggling for time it's nice to have something sweet occasionally. They are also great if you have a last-minute dinner guest who you are trying to impress — people will love you if you make them dessert. I think a lot of life's problems could be solved with a dish such as the fried bananas with salted caramel (see page 58) — it has certainly got me out of the bad books a couple of times!

CHINESE COOKING WINE IS CALLED SHAOHSING OR SHAOXING AND IS AVAILABLE AT ASIAN FOOD SHOPS. IF YOU CAN'T FIND IT, SUBSTITUTE CHICKEN STOCK OR WATER.

This was a great meal I had up my sleeve to make after a long day at uni (assuming you can call a six-hour day starting at 11:00 am long). I love that it's cooked in a wok, which means the ingredients stay fresh and the washing-up is a piece of cake.

MY FAVOURITE STIR-FRY

PREPARATION TIME 10 MINUTES // COOKING TIME 15 MINUTES
SERVES 2 (WITH LEFTOVERS FOR LUNCH)

1. Bring a large saucepan of water to just simmering, reduce the heat to low, add the noodles and cook for 3–4 minutes or until just tender. Drain and place the noodles in cold water to stop them cooking further.
2. Dust the chicken with the five-spice. Heat a wok over high heat, add half of the oil, then add the chicken and stir-fry, tossing occasionally, for 4 minutes or until golden and just cooked. Remove from the wok. Set aside.
3. Add the remaining oil to the wok, then the garlic and chilli. Once the garlic becomes lightly golden, add the broccoli and bok choy. Stir-fry for 2–3 minutes or until the broccoli is bright green and the bok choy has softened. Add the green beans, cooking wine and soy and oyster sauces, and toss around occasionally until the vegetables are cooked to your liking — I like them to be still quite crisp and crunchy.
4. Add the spring onion, along with the chicken to the wok and toss to just warm through.
5. At the last minute, warm your noodles in hot tap water, drain and serve with the stir-fry. Top with the coriander.

270 g (9½ oz) Japanese soba noodles
500 g (1 lb 2 oz) chicken thigh fillets (3 large), diced into 2 cm (¾ inch) pieces
2 teaspoons Chinese five-spice
2 tablespoons vegetable oil
2 garlic cloves, thinly sliced
1 long red chilli, thinly sliced
250 g (9 oz) broccoli (about 1 small head), cut into florets
2 baby bok choy, cut into quarters lengthways
150 g (5½ oz) green beans or snow peas (mangetout), trimmed
2 tablespoons Chinese cooking wine (see opposite)
1½ tablespoons soy sauce, or to taste
60 ml (2 fl oz/¼ cup) oyster sauce, or to taste
3 spring onions (scallions), cut into batons (about 4 cm/1½ inches)
coriander (cilantro) leaves, to serve (optional)

Chicken satay is often served on skewers. Frankly, I find skewers can be fiddly and annoying to eat, so I prefer treating it more like a light curry. Limes are expensive for their size, so make sure you get the most juice out of them by either rolling the whole limes back and forth firmly on a bench or microwaving them for 10 seconds.

SUPER-QUICK CHICKEN SATAY
{WITHOUT THE SKEWERS}

PREPARATION TIME 10 MINUTES // COOKING TIME 15 MINUTES
SERVES 2 (EASILY DOUBLED, JUST COOK IN 2 BATCHES)

400 g (14 oz) chicken thigh fillets
3 teaspoons vegetable oil
60 ml (2 fl oz/¼ cup) coconut milk
150 g (5½ oz) green beans,
    steamed, to serve
cooked rice (see page 31), to serve

SATAY SAUCE
1 garlic clove
1 long red chilli
10 g (⅓ oz) piece of ginger, peeled
    and roughly chopped
70 g (2½ oz/¼ cup) crunchy
    peanut butter
½ bunch coriander (cilantro),
    leaves and stems roughly
    chopped
finely grated zest and juice
    of 1 lime
2 teaspoons fish sauce
    (see right)

1. For the satay sauce, combine the ingredients in a food processor and blend until smooth. Add a little water to help it get to a paste if necessary.
2. Cut each chicken thigh into 3 long strips, then cut each strip into 4 pieces. Get a wok or frying pan nice and hot, then add the oil and when it's hot, add the chicken. Cook for 2 minutes each side or until golden. Don't mess around with it too much or the chicken will sweat instead of browning properly.
3. Add the satay sauce and cook, stirring occasionally, for 3–5 minutes or until slightly darkened in colour and the chicken is almost cooked through. Add the coconut milk and cook for a further minute.
4. Serve with the beans and rice.

FISH SAUCE TAKES A BIT OF GETTING USED TO, BUT IT ADDS A WONDERFUL DEPTH OF FLAVOUR TO DISHES. SQUID BRAND IS REALLY GOOD AND AVAILABLE IN MOST SUPERMARKETS.

KEWPIE MAYONNAISE IS
AVAILABLE IN MOST SUPERMARKETS
IN THE ASIAN FOOD SECTION.

This recipe is from my friend Adam Liaw. He made it for me once, and I have become hooked. It has rapidly become part of my regular diet. Mirin and sake can be found in most Asian supermarkets. Make a bigger batch of the sauce so next time you want to make this dish, the sauce is ready to go — it keeps for ages in the fridge.

TERIYAKI CHICKEN
{THE PROPER WAY!}

PREPARATION TIME 10 MINUTES // COOKING TIME 10 MINUTES // SERVES 2

1. For the teriyaki sauce, combine the ingredients in a small saucepan and stir over low heat until sugar dissolves. Set aside.
2. Heat the oil in a large non-stick frying pan over high heat. Dust the chicken with cornflour, then add to the pan. Cook for 5 minutes, turning once, until golden brown on both sides and just cooked through.
3. Reduce the heat to medium, pour over half the teriyaki sauce and simmer, stirring occasionally, until the sauce thickens and coats the chicken. Pour over the remaining teriyaki sauce, stirring until it thickens again.
4. Sprinkle the sesame seeds and coriander over the chicken and serve with the mayonnaise and a side dish, such as the cucumber and radish salad (see page 159).

1½ tablespoons vegetable oil
400 g (14 oz) chicken thigh fillets, cut into 3 cm (1¼ inch) pieces
1 tablespoon cornflour (cornstarch), for dusting
2 teaspoons sesame seeds
chopped coriander (cilantro) or sliced spring onion (scallion), to serve
Kewpie (Japanese) mayonnaise (see opposite), to serve (optional)

TERIYAKI SAUCE
2½ tablespoons light soy sauce
2 tablespoons sake (Japanese rice wine) or substitute a dry sherry
1½ tablespoons mirin (sweet rice wine)
1 tablespoon caster (superfine) sugar

It might seem weird to use chicken stock in a fish dish, but it's common practice in lots of light seafood dishes because you don't want to overpower the subtle flavours with a dominant fishy taste.

SALMON, LEMON & CAPER FETTUCCINE

PREPARATION TIME 10 MINUTES // COOKING TIME 15 MINUTES // SERVES 2

200 g (7 oz) fettuccine or your
  favourite long pasta
1 tablespoon olive oil
2 garlic cloves, finely chopped
160 ml (5¼ fl oz) chicken stock
160 ml (5¼ fl oz) pouring
  (single) cream
finely grated zest and juice
  of 1 lemon
1 tablespoon baby capers, rinsed
1 tablespoon chopped dill (optional)
200 g (7 oz) smoked salmon, torn
  into bite-sized pieces
finely grated parmesan cheese,
  to serve

1. Bring a large saucepan of salted water to the boil. Add the pasta, stir and cook according to the packet directions or until al dente.
2. Meanwhile, in another large, deep saucepan, heat the olive oil over medium heat and fry the garlic until light golden. Add the chicken stock, increase the heat to high and cook until reduced to 60 ml (2 fl oz/¼ cup). Add the cream and stir to combine. Simmer for 2–3 minutes or until reduced and thickened slightly. Season to taste with salt and pepper.
3. Add the lemon zest and juice, capers and dill to the sauce. Drain the pasta and add to the sauce. Toss around to coat the pasta. Add the salmon and toss to coat. Scatter over the parmesan to serve.

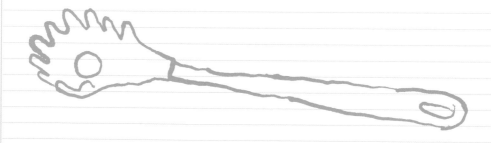

There is a popular Chinese restaurant I always go to when I need a cheap dinner before a night out. I order this dish every time I go, which is saying something because I think tofu is often terrible. If you pair it with strong flavours, though, it's actually really tasty. This is my version, and I think it's a pretty close rendition (other than the missing MSG!).

SALT & PEPPER TOFU

PREPARATION TIME 10 MINUTES // COOKING TIME 15 MINUTES
SERVES 1 HUNGRY BLOKE OR 2–4 AS PART OF A SHARED MEAL OR BANQUET

1. For the soy dipping sauce, combine all the ingredients in a small bowl.
2. Heat the oil in a wok to 180°C (350°F) or until a cube of bread turns golden in 15 seconds. Cut the tofu into 2 cm (¾ inch) cubes. Use paper towel to pat dry any excess moisture. Coat with the cornflour and shake off any excess. Add half of the tofu to the oil and deep-fry for 5 minutes or until golden and crisp. Remove, using a slotted spoon, shaking carefully over the wok to remove any excess oil. Place in a large bowl, season generously with the salt and pepper and toss gently to combine. Repeat with the remaining tofu. Set aside.
3. Take the wok off the heat and allow the oil to cool before pouring into a metal bowl, leaving 2 teaspoons of oil in the wok.
4. Heat the wok over medium–high heat, add the spring onion, chilli and garlic and stir-fry until golden. Add the tofu back to the wok and toss to combine and warm through. Pile the tofu onto a plate. Serve with the soy dipping sauce.

1 litre (35 fl oz/4 cups) vegetable oil, for deep-frying
350 g (12 oz) packet firm tofu
2 tablespoons cornflour (cornstarch)
sea salt and freshly ground black pepper
3 spring onions (scallions), thinly sliced on an angle
1 long red chilli, thinly sliced
1 garlic clove, thinly sliced

SOY DIPPING SAUCE
2 tablespoons light soy sauce
2 tablespoons mirin (sweet rice wine) (see below)
2 teaspoons rice wine vinegar
½ teaspoon grated ginger

MIRIN IS FOUND IN THE ASIAN SECTION OF MOST SUPERMARKETS.

YELLOW FISH CURRY

PREPARATION TIME 15 MINUTES // COOKING TIME 15 MINUTES // SERVES 4

180 ml (5⅔ fl oz) coconut cream
400 ml (14 fl oz) coconut milk
2 tablespoons fish sauce
1 tablespoon chopped palm sugar
   (jaggery)
2 tablespoons lime juice
250 g (9 oz) cherry tomatoes,
   halved
150 g (5½ oz) snow peas
   (mangetout), stringy bits
   removed
500 g (1 lb 2 oz) skinless snapper,
   ling or other white fish, cut
   into 3 cm (1¼ inch) dice
coriander (cilantro) leaves, to serve
cooked rice (see page 31), to serve

CURRY PASTE
4 French shallots (eschalots),
   roughly chopped
25 g (1 oz) piece of ginger, peeled
   and sliced
4 garlic cloves, roughly chopped
2 long red chillies, seeds removed
   if you want the curry mild,
   roughly chopped
½ bunch coriander (cilantro),
   stems and roots only
   (see right), washed and
   roughly chopped
2 lemongrass stalks, white part
   only, sliced
2 teaspoons shrimp paste (optional)
½ teaspoon ground turmeric
2 tablespoons vegetable oil

1. For the curry paste, combine all the ingredients, except the oil in a food processor, and blend until finely chopped. While the machine is running, add just enough oil to make a smooth paste.

2. Heat a wok or large saucepan over medium heat. Add just the thick top layer from the tin of coconut cream and cook, stirring, until it splits and looks oily rather than creamy. Add the curry paste and stir-fry for 3 minutes or until the fragrance has mellowed and darkened in colour. Add the remaining coconut cream and the coconut milk. Stir to combine.

3. Add the fish sauce, palm sugar and lime juice (best to add the amounts specified, taste, then adjust to get the correct balance of sweet, salty and sour). Add the cherry tomatoes, snow peas and fish and simmer for 2–3 minutes or until the fish is just cooked through.

4. Scatter with the coriander. I like to give everyone a bowl with some rice in it, put the curry in the middle of the table and let people go nuts.

> CUT THE CORIANDER STEMS JUST ABOVE WHERE THEY JOIN THE ROOT AS THERE IS ALWAYS DIRT TRAPPED IN THAT AREA. STEM REFERS TO THE WHOLE STALK UP TO WHERE THE LEAVES START.

This is my go-to last-minute dessert and is great eaten as is with fruit, but it can also be used as a filling to sandwich layered cakes or as a component of another dessert. Unlike most chocolate mousses, you can eat it straight away because you don't need to wait for any gelatine or eggs to set. If you put it in the fridge, though, it goes quite hard, so I tend to make only a small amount and eat it straight away. What's great about this dish is that it looks like you have gone to more effort than you actually have.

FIVE-MINUTE CHOCOLATE MOUSSE

PREPARATION TIME 15 MINUTES // COOKING TIME 5 MINUTES
SERVES 2 (EASILY DOUBLED OR TRIPLED TO FEED AN ARMY)

250 ml (9 fl oz/1 cup) thickened (whipping) cream
200 g (7 oz) good-quality dark chocolate, broken into small pieces

1. In a large bowl, use electric beaters or an energetic whisking arm to whip the cream to firm peaks. (Sometimes it's a good idea to tag-team with a friend if whisking by hand.)
2. Put the chocolate in a heatproof bowl over a small saucepan of just-simmering water. Make sure the bowl is not touching the water below. Stir the chocolate with a metal spoon until melted. Remove from the heat and allow to cool for 1 minute. (Alternatively, melt the chocolate in a microwave on medium–high power in 10-second bursts, stirring between each burst, until smooth.)
3. Pour the chocolate onto the cream, whisking gently the whole time to incorporate well. Serve immediately.

It sounds unusual to have salt in a dessert, but salt balances the sugar, acting to make the sugar less sweet. Think of sweet things such as Snickers bars: completely loaded with salt — delicious though! If you're not sold on the idea, wait until the very end to add the salt. Taste a little bit, then add the salt and taste again. Make up your own mind. Any left-over caramel will happily sit in your fridge. It will go a bit hard, so just reheat it in a saucepan or in the microwave. Use on ice cream, to top cupcakes or eat with a spoon while on a long phone conversation (I've certainly never done that). This recipe can easily be doubled — just cook two more bananas in another frying pan or in two batches.

FRIED BANANAS WITH SALTED CARAMEL

PREPARATION TIME 10 MINUTES // COOKING TIME 15 MINUTES // SERVES 2

2 medium relatively firm bananas
100 g (3½ oz) butter
125 ml (4 fl oz/½ cup) thickened (whipping) cream
165 g (5¾ oz/¾ cup firmly packed) soft brown sugar
½ teaspoon salt
vanilla ice cream, to serve
2 tablespoons roughly chopped hazelnuts, to serve

1. Cut the bananas in half lengthways. Heat a large non-stick frying pan over medium heat. Add 2 tablespoons of the butter, then add the bananas, cut side down, and cook for 2 minutes or until golden. Carefully flip over and cook for a further 2 minutes or until evenly coloured. Transfer to serving plates.

2. Add the remaining butter, cream, sugar and salt to the pan and stir. Once the butter has melted and the sugar has dissolved, whack up the heat and simmer for 3–5 minutes or until thickened and smooth, stirring now and then. Don't cook the caramel for too long or it will start to burn.

3. Pour some caramel over the bananas, top with a couple of big scoops of ice cream and scatter over the hazelnuts.

JUST LIKE MUM MAKES

This chapter is devoted to the style of food I grew up eating.
I was going to call this chapter 'Just Like Dad Makes' because
my dad did a lot of the cooking, but it didn't have the same
ring to it. I'm pretty superficial like that. I think it's great to
know how to cook a good roast or make a knockout chocolate
pudding but thankfully our culture has moved away from the
meat 'n' three veg that it once was. We've now incorporated
little bits and pieces of cuisine from a lot of countries to give
us a great variety of dishes to eat.

A PRETTY SWELL MINESTRONE

PREPARATION TIME 15 MINUTES // COOKING TIME 40 MINUTES // SERVES 4–6

1. In the biggest saucepan that you own, add the oil and place over medium heat. Once it's pretty hot, add the bacon and cook, stirring, for 5 minutes or until browned. Add the onion, carrot and celery and cook, stirring now and then, for 5 minutes or until the onion softens. Add the garlic and continue to stir occasionally until the ingredients look golden brown. This will take a few minutes.

2. Pour in the tomatoes, beef stock, 500 ml (17 fl oz/2 cups) of water and season to taste with pepper. Simmer for 20 minutes or until the vegetables are cooked through (depending on how big you dice the veg).

3. Add the macaroni and cook for 5 minutes. You want the broccoli to stay nice and green, rather than turn grey, so add this along with the cannellini beans when the pasta is almost cooked. If desired, add some chopped parsley at this point. Season to taste with salt.

4. For the pesto, preheat the oven to 180°C (350°F/Gas 4). Lay the pine nuts on a baking tray and roast for 5 minutes or until lightly golden. Allow to cool completely, then combine with the basil leaves, garlic and a pinch of salt in the bowl of a food processor. Process until finely chopped. While the machine is running, pour in the oil. Scrape into a bowl and stir in the parmesan.

5. Serve the soup with some crusty bread and the pesto, or cheese and mustard on toast if you like.

1 tablespoon extra virgin olive oil
3 bacon rashers (185 g/6½ oz), rind removed and chopped
1 brown onion, diced
1 carrot, diced
1 celery stalk, diced
2 garlic cloves, sliced
400 g (14 oz) tin chopped tomatoes
1 litre (35 fl oz/4 cups) beef stock, made from cubes
100 g (3½ oz/⅔ cup) macaroni
150 g (5½ oz) broccoli (about 1 small head), chopped into florets
400 g (14 oz) tin cannellini (white) beans, drained and rinsed
½ cup flat-leaf (Italian) parsley leaves, chopped (optional)
crusty bread, to serve

PESTO
40 g (1½ oz/¼ cup) pine nuts
1 cup basil leaves
1 garlic clove, crushed
60 ml (2 fl oz/¼ cup) olive oil
35 g (1¼ oz/¼ cup) finely grated parmesan cheese

CRISPY CRUMBED FISH WITH QUICK TARTARE SAUCE

PREPARATION TIME 15 MINUTES // COOKING TIME 15 MINUTES // SERVES 4

½ teaspoon salt

plain (all-purpose) flour,
     for dusting

2 eggs

60 g (2¼ oz/1 cup) panko
     (Japanese) breadcrumbs

4 x 100 g (3½ oz) skinless white
     fish fillets, such as hake,
     snapper, flathead or basa

olive or vegetable oil, for
     shallow-frying

chips (see page 169), to serve

lemon wedges, to serve

QUICK TARTARE

150 g (5½ oz) good-quality
     mayonnaise

1 tablespoon chopped flat-leaf
     (Italian) parsley

1 tablespoon chopped baby capers

1 tablespoon pickled gherkins
     (AKA cornichons)

finely grated zest and juice
     of ½ lemon

1. For the quick tartare, combine all the ingredients in a small bowl and set aside. Get three big plates or flat bowls. Mix the salt and flour together in one, crack the eggs into another and put the breadcrumbs in the last. Use a fork to beat the eggs a little. Dip a fish fillet into the flour, shaking off any excess. Transfer the fillet to the beaten egg and coat, then put the fillet into the breadcrumbs and make sure it is covered everywhere. Repeat with the remaining fillets. You can do up to this step earlier in the day if you want and just refrigerate until needed.

2. Place a large frying pan over medium–high heat and fill with enough oil to come 5 mm (¼ inch) up the side. You want the oil hot but not smoking. Add two of the fish fillets. You want a good sizzle so that the fish cooks quickly and the crumbs turn golden brown. Cook for about 3 minutes, then carefully turn over with a fish slice and cook until the other side is golden. Don't use tongs to turn the fish or it will break apart. Remove and drain any excess oil on paper towel. Repeat with the other fillets.

3. Serve the fish with the tartare, chips, lemon wedges, and the fennel, orange and walnut salad (see page 160). Or serve the fish and chips in a newspaper cone for a retro feel.

I used to make stuffing for my roast chicken until I came across Jamie Oliver's method of using a lemon. It's way quicker (and I've never been too fussed on stuffing anyway). If you've never made gravy from scratch before, give it a go. If you really still can't be bothered and want to make it from packet stuff, at least pour the pan juices into the gravy to give it some real chickeny flavour. (Chickeny is in the *Oxford Dictionary* and is most certainly a word. I'm so confident of this fact I insist you don't check whether I'm right or wrong. I'm not entirely sure who let me write a book; my editor is eventually going to go crazy and beat me senseless with a laptop. I'm sure of it.)

ROAST CHICKEN WITH REAL GRAVY

PREPARATION TIME 30 MINUTES // COOKING TIME 1 HOUR 25 MINUTES // SERVES 4

1 x 1.8 kg (4 lb) chicken
    (preferably free-range)
1 lemon
1 teaspoon thyme leaves
2 teaspoons crushed garlic
2 tablespoons olive oil
¼ teaspoon salt
freshly ground black pepper
3 brown onions, halved

REAL GRAVY
1 tablespoon plain (all-purpose)
    flour
2 tablespoons dry white wine
1 litre (35 fl oz/4 cups) good-quality
    low-salt chicken stock
40 g (1½ oz) butter, cut into a
    few pieces

1. Preheat the oven to 190°C (375°F/Gas 5). Rinse the chicken and pat dry with paper towel. Finely grate the lemon zest into a small bowl. Add the thyme leaves, garlic, olive oil, salt and pepper and stir to combine. Rub the mixture all over the chicken, leaving the chunky bits of the marinade mostly on the breasts. Pierce the zested lemon several times with a sharp knife and push it into the chicken cavity. (If you have some extra thyme sprigs, shove them in too.)
2. Arrange the onion halves, cut side down, in the middle of a flameproof roasting tray lined with baking paper and sit the chicken on top. Roast for 1 hour 10 minutes or until just cooked. To test, use a skewer or small sharp knife to prick the inside of the leg where the thigh meets the body. Pull the leg away a little — the juices that run out should be clear, not pink or bloody.
3. When the chicken is cooked, transfer to a chopping board, breast side down, and leave to rest for 10 minutes. This allows the chicken breasts to suck up all the juices and ensures the meat is moist and tender.
4. Meanwhile, make your gravy. Pour out any excess fat from the roasting tray so you are left with only about 2 tablespoons. Place the tray over high heat on the stovetop, add the flour to the fat and stir with a wooden spoon, scraping up any stuck-on bits. Mush the onion around a bit too. Once the flour has cooked for about 2 minutes, add the wine. Once it has nearly all bubbled away, add 60 ml (2 fl oz/¼ cup) of the stock and whisk until lump-free. Add the remaining stock and bring to the boil, whisking continuously until well combined and the gravy has thickened. Whisk in the butter (pass the gravy through a fine sieve if you don't want lumps).
5. To carve the chicken, cut it in half lengthways straight down the centre of the breast, cutting through the ribs just next to the spine. Turn one of the halves, so it's cut side down, lift the leg slightly and cut on an angle to separate the leg from the breast, so you have a leg-and-thigh piece and a breast-and-wing piece. Repeat with the other half and serve with the gravy.

Roast chicken page 66

Individual chicken and mushroom pies page 70

These little pies are full of flavour and pretty rich, so it's a good idea to serve them with a salad or something refreshing. You could make one big pie if you don't have ramekins — the cooking time will be about the same as the filling is already cooked and you just need to brown the pastry.

INDIVIDUAL CHICKEN & MUSHROOM PIES

PREPARATION TIME 30 MINUTES // COOKING TIME 50 MINUTES PLUS COOLING TIME
SERVES 4

1 tablespoon olive oil

3 middle bacon rashers, rind removed and thinly sliced

700 g (1 lb 9 oz) chicken thigh fillets, cut into 2 cm (¾ inch) dice

2 tablespoons plain (all-purpose) flour

300 g (10½ oz) Swiss brown or button mushrooms, quartered (cut any large mushrooms into more pieces)

3 garlic cloves, finely chopped

30 g (1 oz) butter

1 teaspoon thyme leaves

finely grated zest of 1 orange

60 ml (2 fl oz/¼ cup) white wine

10 g (⅓ oz) dried porcini mushrooms, soaked in 2 tablespoons hot water (optional) (see below)

250 ml (9 fl oz/1 cup) good-quality chicken stock

1 sheet frozen puff pastry, thawed

1 egg, lightly beaten

DRIED PORCINI MUSHROOMS
ARE AVAILABLE FROM DELIS,
FRUIT AND VEG STORES AND
SOME SUPERMARKETS.

1. Preheat the oven to 220°C (425°F/Gas 7).
2. Heat the oil in a large heavy-based saucepan over high heat. Add the bacon and cook for 2 minutes or until golden, then remove, leaving the fat in the pan.
3. Season the flour with salt and pepper. Add the chicken pieces and toss lightly to coat. Add the chicken to the pan and cook for 5 minutes or until golden on all sides. Add the Swiss brown mushrooms and cook, stirring occasionally, for 5 minutes or until browned.
4. Add the garlic and stir. Add the butter, thyme leaves and orange zest and stir to combine. Once the butter has melted and foamed, add the white wine and allow to bubble until the liquid has almost all evaporated. If using porcini mushrooms, roughly chop and add them to the pan along with the water they were soaked in.
5. Reduce the heat to medium and return the bacon to the pan. Pour in the stock and simmer, stirring occasionally, for 5 minutes or until it reduces and thickens to a gravy. Remove from the heat and taste for seasoning.
6. You will need four 250 ml (9 fl oz/1 cup) capacity ramekins (see above). Use one of them as a stencil to cut out four circles from the pastry with a knife, making sure the circles are 1 cm (½ inch) larger all around. Using a pastry brush, moisten the top edge of each ramekin with the beaten egg. Evenly fill the ramekins with the mixture and flatten with the back of a spoon. Place a circle of pastry on the rim of each ramekin, brush the pastry lids with the beaten egg and make a small cross with a knife in each to allow the steam to escape. Bake for 20–25 minutes or until golden brown. Allow to cool for 5 minutes before serving.

Bolognese is one of the first meals I remember eating. There has to be a million recipes for it. This is the one I use. By all means change it to suit your own tastes, and if you miss out one of the veggies or just use one type of mince, so be it. You can use this recipe for a whole bunch of dishes, and I have included my favourites on pages 73–75. It's worthwhile making a big batch of it as it refrigerates and freezes well, so a future dinner is never far away.

THREE WAYS WITH BOLOGNESE

PREPARATION TIME 20 MINUTES // COOKING TIME 35 MINUTES

2 tablespoons olive oil
3 rashers bacon, rind removed
    and sliced
2 brown onions, finely chopped
1 large carrot, finely chopped
1 celery stalk, finely chopped
3 garlic cloves, sliced
2 tablespoons tomato paste
    (concentrated purée)
300 g (10½ oz) minced
    (ground) veal or beef
300 g (10½ oz) minced
    (ground) pork
125 ml (4 fl oz/½ cup) red wine
2 x 400 g (14 oz) tins chopped
    tomatoes

1. In your largest heavy-based saucepan, heat the oil over medium heat, add the bacon and cook for 2–3 minutes or until golden. Add the onion, carrot, celery and garlic and cook, stirring with a wooden spoon occasionally, for 5 minutes or until the vegetables have softened. Add the tomato paste and cook, stirring, for a further 2 minutes.

2. Increase the heat to high, add all the meat and use the spoon or a potato masher to squish the mince and separate the chunks. Add the wine and let it simmer away for a few seconds, then add the tomatoes. Simmer for 20 minutes or until thickened but not stodgy. Season generously with salt and pepper.

Béchamel is that thick gloopy white sauce in lasagne.
It takes a while to make, and is a bit boring. I think it tastes like flour,
regardless of how much you try and cook it out. If you use mozzarella
and crème fraîche instead, you get a quicker (and tastier!) result. Crème
fraîche was once difficult to find but most supermarkets sell it now.

NO-BÉCHAMEL LASAGNE

PREPARATION TIME 15 MINUTES // COOKING TIME 30 MINUTES // SERVES 4

1. Preheat the oven to 190°C (375°F/Gas 5).
2. To assemble the lasagne, find yourself a
   baking dish and spread one-third of the
   Bolognese sauce over the base. Cover with
   enough lasagne sheets to form one layer
   (feel free to tear or cut the sheets to make
   them fit) Spoon over one-third of the crème
   fraîche. Use the back of the spoon to move
   it around so it covers the lasagne sheets
   somewhat evenly, then sprinkle over one-
   third of the mozzarella. Repeat twice more
   with the remaining ingredients, finishing
   with a layer of lasagne sheets. Top with
   the the extra mozzarella, the parmesan
   and a little pepper.
3. Bake for 30 minutes or until the pasta is
   cooked and the cheese is golden brown.
   Allow to cool for 5 minutes before slicing
   and serving.

1 quantity Bolognese sauce
  (see opposite)
375 g (13 oz) packet fresh lasagne
  sheets
400 g (14 oz) crème fraîche
125 g (4½ oz/1 cup) coarsely
  grated mozzarella cheese,
  plus 65 g (2⅓ oz/½ cup) extra,
  for the top
70 g (2½ oz/½ cup) finely grated
  parmesan cheese
freshly ground black pepper

Rich Bolognese sauce topped with a thick layer of creamy mashed potato is what dreams are made of. That's probably going a bit far, but give me a big serving of shepherd's pie and you'll win me over every day of the week.

SHEPHERD'S PIE

PREPARATION TIME 15 MINUTES // COOKING TIME 30 MINUTES // SERVES 4–6

1. Preheat the oven to 200°C (400°F/Gas 6).
2. Pour the Bolognese sauce into a 3 litre (105 fl oz) capacity ovenproof dish (or individual ramekins). Top with the mashed potato, sprinkle over the parmesan and bake for 20 minutes or until the cheese has melted. Allow to cool for 5 minutes before serving.

1 quantity Bolognese sauce (see page 72)
1 quantity basic mashed potato (see page 168)
70 g (2½ oz/½ cup) finely grated parmesan cheese

SPAG BOL

PREPARATION TIME 5 MINUTES // COOKING TIME 10 MINUTES // SERVES 4

1. Bring a large saucepan of salted water to the boil. Add the pasta, stir and cook according to the packet directions or until al dente. Drain and toss through the Bolognese sauce.
2. Stir through the basil leaves and half the parmesan. Divide into serving bowls and top with the remaining parmesan.

1 quantity Bolognese sauce (see page 72)
400 g (14 oz) dried spaghetti
½ cup basil leaves
70 g (2½ oz/½ cup) finely grated parmesan cheese

I grew up more or less in a vegetarian household because my sister was veg. This dish rapidly became a family favourite. It's simple to make, the flavours are really pleasing, and I think Mum liked that we were eating spinach.

SPINACH & RICOTTA CANNELLONI

PREPARATION TIME 25 MINUTES // COOKING TIME 45 MINUTES
SERVES 2 (WITH LOTS OF YUMMY LEFTOVERS) OR 4 WITH A SALAD

250 g (9 oz) baby spinach
500 g (1 lb 2 oz) fresh ricotta cheese (see below)
35 g (1¼ oz/¼ cup) finely grated parmesan cheese
75 g (2⅔ oz/¾ cup) grated cheddar cheese
2 egg yolks
3 teaspoons crushed garlic
finely grated zest of 1 large lemon
16 dried cannelloni pasta tubes
690 g (1 lb 8½ oz) tomato passata (puréed tomatoes) or pasta sauce (have an extra bottle on hand in case)

> RICOTTA IS BEST FROM THE DELI SECTION OF THE SUPERMARKET.

1. Preheat the oven to 180°C (350°F/Gas 4).
2. First, make the filling. Get a big pot of boiling water and plunge the spinach into it. After a few seconds, it will wilt. At this point, drain the spinach and run cold water over it to stop it cooking any further. This step is not essential but it cools the spinach down quickly, making it easier to fill the cannelloni tubes. Squeeze the excess moisture from the spinach, roughly chop and place in a big bowl.
3. Mix in the ricotta, parmesan, one-third of the cheddar, the egg yolks, garlic, lemon zest and a generous pinch of salt and pepper. Using a spoon, your finger or a piping (icing) bag, fill the cannelloni tubes with the spinach mixture. Make sure you fill them to the brim. Find a baking dish that is suitable to go into the oven and will fit the cannelloni tubes snugly in one layer (a 3 litre/105 fl oz capacity one is ideal) and pour in enough passata to cover its base. Arrange the filled tubes so they fit snugly, then pour over the remaining passata to cover. If they're not fully covered, use some of that spare bottle of passata. Top with the remaining cheddar and bake for 40–45 minutes or until the pasta is soft when pierced with a knife.

BEEF & PUMPKIN TAGINE

PREPARATION TIME 30 MINUTES // COOKING TIME 2½ HOURS // SERVES 4

2½ tablespoons olive oil

1 kg (2 lb 4 oz) chuck steak, trimmed and cut into 3 cm (1¼ inch) pieces

2 red onions, cut into wedges

3 garlic cloves, crushed

1 tablespoon ground cumin

1 tablespoon ground coriander

1 tablespoon sweet paprika

2 teaspoons ground cinnamon

1 litre (35 fl oz/4 cups) good-quality beef stock

500 g (1 lb 2 oz) butternut pumpkin (winter squash), peeled and seeds removed, cut into 1.5 cm (⅝ inch) dice

85 g (3 oz/½ cup) raisins

1 tablespoon honey

190 g (6¾ oz/1 cup) instant couscous

¼ cup flaked or slivered almonds, toasted (see below)

¼ cup coriander (cilantro) or flat-leaf (Italian) parsley leaves

1. Preheat the oven to 150°C (300°F/Gas 2).

2. Heat 2 tablespoons of the oil in a large casserole dish or ovenproof heavy-based saucepan over high heat. Season the steak with a pinch of salt, then add one-third of the meat to the pan. Cook for 2 minutes each side or until browned. Remove and set aside. Repeat with the remaining meat in batches.

3. Reduce the heat to medium, add the onion and garlic to the pan and cook, stirring, for 5 minutes or until the onion is soft. Add the spices and cook for 1 minute. Add the meat back to the pan and give it a good stir. Pour in the stock and bring to a simmer. Cover with a lid and cook in the oven for 1½ hours or until the beef is very tender.

4. Carefully remove the pan from the oven, add the pumpkin, raisins and honey, give it a good stir and return to the oven for another 30 minutes or until the pumpkin is soft. If the sauce is still really thin, place on the stovetop and simmer, uncovered, until thickened.

5. Meanwhile, place the couscous in a large heatproof bowl and rub in the remaining oil. Pour 250 ml (9 fl oz/1 cup) of boiled water over the couscous, leave for 1 minute, then fluff with a fork, repeating every few minutes until lump-free. Season with salt and pepper.

6. Place the couscous bowl over the saucepan, stirring now and then to warm through. Serve the tagine, scattered with the almonds and coriander leaves, with the couscous.

> TO TOAST ALMONDS, SCATTER THEM OVER A BAKING TRAY AND ROAST IN A 180°C (350°F/GAS 4) OVEN FOR 5 MINUTES OR UNTIL GOLDEN.

This was one of my favourite childhood rituals, which would take place at my mate Kyle's house after a basketball game. We would be starving, so Kyle's mum would make us a pasta bake followed by chocolate pudding with ice cream. I have no idea how we got through it all — the pudding was a packet mix designed to serve six! This is my version — it's like a chocolate fondant, so it should be set around the outside and soft in the middle. Make sure you use dark chocolate as milk chocolate will be far too sweet.

KYLE'S MUM'S GOOEY CHOCOLATE PUDDINGS

PREPARATION TIME 20 MINUTES // COOKING TIME 20 MINUTES // MAKES 4

1. Preheat the oven to 180°C (350°F/Gas 4). Lightly grease with butter four 310 ml (10¾ fl oz/1¼ cup) capacity ceramic ramekins.
2. Melt the chocolate and butter in a metal bowl over a saucepan of simmering water — make sure the bowl does not touch the water below. Lightly whisk together the eggs, egg yolks and sugar. Do not overmix or the puddings will rise, then collapse when baked.
3. Whisk the chocolate into the egg mixture until combined. Fold in the flour. Pour into the ramekins to two-thirds full. (You can do up to this stage in advance and just store in the fridge. The puddings will take longer to cook if refrigerated.)
4. Bake for 10–14 minutes or until the edges are set but there is still a slight wobble in the middle, but no moistness on top. Sit and cool in the ramekins for 2 minutes before serving with a big scoop of ice cream.

50 g (1¾ oz) unsalted butter, chopped, plus extra for greasing
150 g (5½ oz) good-quality dark chocolate (preferably 70% cocoa solids), chopped
3 eggs
3 egg yolks
170 g (6 oz) caster (superfine) sugar
2 tablespoons plain (all-purpose) flour
vanilla ice cream, to serve

Don't be put off by the name — these are a far cry from the ho-hum tinned version of baked beans. Awesome for breakfast or dinner, I like them served with a poached egg or maybe some sliced avocado on toast. Okay, so these beans are not really all that *Greek* (and they're not even baked if you want to get right down to it), so make sure you put the feta on top to give it at least a little bit of authenticity.

GREEK BAKED BEANS

PREPARATION TIME 20 MINUTES // COOKING TIME 20 MINUTES // SERVES 4

1. In a large saucepan, heat the oil over medium heat. Add the bacon and once golden, add the carrot, celery, onion and garlic. Cook, stirring occasionally, until the onion is translucent. Add the tomatoes and simmer for 10 minutes or until the mixture is no longer watery and has thickened.
2. Stir in the beans and season with a generous pinch of salt and pepper. Scatter over the feta and parsley and serve with toasted bread.

1 tablespoon olive oil

3 streaky bacon rashers, rind removed and sliced about 5 mm (¼ inch) thick

1 carrot, finely chopped

1 celery stalk, finely chopped

1 brown onion, diced

2 garlic cloves, thinly sliced

2 x 400 g (14 oz) tins chopped tomatoes

2 x 400 g (14 oz) tins beans (such as cannellini/white, butterbeans/lima or even chickpeas), drained and rinsed

100 g (3½ oz) feta cheese, crumbled, to serve

½ cup flat-leaf (Italian) parsley leaves, chopped

toasted bread, to serve

The best part about this ice-cream recipe is that you don't need an ice-cream maker to make it; you get a beautiful creamy result by just chucking it in the freezer. This is a family favourite. I think mostly because it was simple enough for my sister and me to make as kids. It's pretty versatile — we often made 'hokey pokey' ice cream by replacing the biscuits with bashed-up chocolate-honeycomb bars. You could use anything you have lurking around really. (Well, that's not quite true; I wouldn't chuck in a rack of lamb!) Other delicious additions, such as your favourite nuts or perhaps the pulp of 6–8 passionfruit, would work swimmingly too.

COOKIES 'N' CREAM ICE CREAM

PREPARATION TIME 10 MINUTES PLUS 3–4 HOURS FREEZING // COOKING TIME NIL
SERVES 4–6

600 ml (21 fl oz) thickened (whipping) cream

395 g (13¾ oz) tin sweetened condensed milk

150 g (5½ oz) chocolate biscuits (I like to use Oreos)

1. In a large bowl, whip the cream to soft peaks, then whisk in the condensed milk.
2. Place the biscuits in a zip-lock bag, then lightly bash with a rolling pin or saucepan until roughly crushed. Fold the crushed biscuit into the cream mixture. Transfer to a freezer-safe container and freeze for 3–4 hours. It keeps well for quite a few days.

COOKING FOR A CROWD

Cooking for other people is one of my favourite things to do. I think of food as much more than something that gives you energy; it has the ability to bring people together. Think of any major occasion: my best memories of Christmas aren't of the presents but are of gathering around a big table with the people I love. When I was sixteen, my dad passed away and people didn't really know what to say, so they tried to help out with food — I don't think I have ever seen so many casseroles or baked goods in my life! There are not too many things that everyone has in common, but we all have to eat.

This chapter contains recipes suitable for cooking for a number of people. Lots of the dishes are the type for which cutlery isn't necessary, so the food is pretty informal, which is great for having some friends over for a good feed. Or it might be having something sweet on a casual Sunday arvo, cooking a big pot of something warm for your housemate on a weeknight, or having a burrito feast before a big Saturday night out.

Put some of these out for your friends, they'll love you for it! Just make sure you have a couple of cold beers on hand as they can be a little spicy. There's no need for cutlery here — it's a good chance to get your hands dirty!

FIERY STICKY CHICKEN WINGS

PREPARATION TIME 20 MINUTES PLUS 2 HOURS MARINATING
COOKING TIME 45 MINUTES // SERVES 4 AS A LIGHT SNACK

1 kg (2 lb 4 oz) chicken wings

MARINADE
60 ml (2 fl oz/¼ cup) tomato
    sauce (ketchup)
2 tablespoons firmly packed
    soft brown sugar
60 ml (2 fl oz/¼ cup) soy sauce
1 tablespoon smoked paprika
1 tablespoon ground cumin
1 tablespoon ground coriander
1½ teaspoons chilli powder
½ teaspoon freshly ground
    black pepper
½ teaspoon salt
2 tablespoons Dijon mustard

1. Whisk all the marinade ingredients together in a small bowl or jug.
2. Place the chicken wings in a shallow, non-reactive (i.e. non-metal) dish and pour the marinade over the top. Cover with plastic wrap and refrigerate for 2 hours, turning over whenever you remember to.
3. Preheat the oven to 210°C (415°F/Gas 6–7). Pick up the wings from the marinade and transfer to a large baking dish — try to keep them in a single layer, not stacked on top of each other, to ensure even cooking. Bake for 40–45 minutes or until the chicken is cooked through. Turn the chicken wings halfway through the cooking time, and baste them with left-over marinade during cooking if you like, but I usually forget.

IF YOU DON'T HAVE A FOOD
PROCESSOR, YOU CAN MAKE
THE MAYONNAISE WITH A
WHISK AND A BOWL. JUST
PUT A CURLED-UP DAMP TEA
TOWEL UNDER YOUR BOWL SO
YOU HAVE TWO HANDS FREE
TO WHISK AND POUR OIL.
BE WARNED, WHISKING BY
HAND IS QUITE A WORKOUT!

When making mayo, if you add the oil too quickly, it will look split. If this does happen, set aside the split mixture. Combine 1 egg yolk with 1 teaspoon of mustard in the food processor. Blend together, then slowly pour in the split mixture until it thickens.

SKEWERED PRAWNS WITH LIME & SESAME MAYO

PREPARATION TIME 20 MINUTES // COOKING TIME 5 MINUTES
SERVES 10 AS A SNACK OR CANAPÉ (THIS RECIPE EASILY DOUBLES OR TRIPLES)

1. For the mayo, combine the egg yolks, mustard and lime juice with a pinch of salt in a small food processor (see opposite). Blend for 30 seconds or until smooth and slightly increased in volume. With the machine running, add the oil in a very slow, steady stream until the mayonnaise is white and thick. I'm being serious when I say a really slow stream. It should just about be drop-by-drop to start with, then you can pour a bit faster after you have added half the oil. Keep adding oil until the mayonnaise becomes nice and thick — you will need more or less depending on the size of the eggs. Blend in the sesame oil and season to taste.

2. Thread a prawn onto each skewer. Preheat a frying pan, chargrill (griddle) pan or barbecue to full heat. Lightly brush with the oil, then cook the prawns for 1 minute each side or until just cooked through. Season with salt. Transer to a platter and evenly scatter the sesame seeds over the top. Serve with the mayonnaise and the lime cheeks.

30 small skewers
30 raw large prawns (shrimp), peeled and deveined (if the tails are attached that's okay)
2 tablespoons vegetable oil
1 teaspoon toasted white sesame seeds
1 teaspoon toasted black sesame seeds
lime cheeks, to serve

LIME & SESAME MAYO
2 egg yolks
2 teaspoons Dijon mustard
1½ tablespoons lime juice
250 ml (9 fl oz/1 cup) vegetable oil
¼ teaspoon sesame oil

PULLED PORK BUNS WITH NO-MAYO SLAW

PREPARATION TIME 15 MINUTES // COOKING TIME 3 HOURS // MAKES 12

1.5 kg (3 lb 5 oz) boneless pork
    scotch roast, skin on
2 teaspoons salt
2 tablespoons vegetable oil
hoisin sauce (see method), plus
    extra to serve

NO-MAYO SLAW
½ Chinese cabbage (wombok)
3 carrots
3 spring onions (scallions)
3 quantities Thai dressing
    (see page 156)

TO SERVE
12 soft white buns
1 Lebanese (short) cucumber,
    thinly sliced
Kewpie (Japanese) mayonnaise
    (optional) (see opposite)

1. Preheat the oven to 180°C (350°F/Gas 4). Line your largest roasting tray with two excessively long pieces of foil. Pat the pork with paper towel to get rid of any excess moisture. Rub the pork all over with the salt and a little vegetable oil. Place in the tray and wrap tightly with the foil. Roast for 3 hours or until the meat is falling apart. Let the meat cool slightly, then remove any skin, cartilage or excess fat. Shred the meat using two forks.

2. Now for a little bit of maths: you want about a 1:5 ratio of hoisin sauce to shredded meat or, in other words, 20 per cent hoisin. So after removing all the skin, fat and whatnot, I was left with 800 g (1 lb 12 oz) shredded pork meat. Twenty per cent of 800 g is 160 g (5⅔ oz), so I added 160 g hoisin sauce and stirred to combine. (Alternatively, screw the maths and pour in enough hoisin until it tastes good.)

3. For the slaw, cut off most of the white stem of the cabbage and discard. Roll up a few leaves at a time, like a big cigar, and slice as thin as you can. Use a mandoline or a grater to cut the carrot into thin matchsticks. Slice the spring onions on an angle. Gently toss together all the vegetables with the dressing.

4. To serve, cut the burger buns in half and lightly toast under a grill (broiler). Top with the pork and slaw, and add some cucumber, mayo and extra hoisin sauce.

KEWPIE MAYONNAISE CAN
BE FOUND IN THE ASIAN FOOD
SECTION OF MOST SUPERMARKETS.

I could eat bowl after bowl of this soup. It's basically a Chinese chicken noodle soup, but for me it's not really about the chicken or the noodles, it's about the broth. All the aromatic ingredients leave you with an intensely flavoured broth, which is delicious in its own right and can be used as a chicken stock in a lot of other dishes. Try adding a little left-over stock to a stir-fry to help it steam — it adds a whole lot of flavour.

CAL'S FAVE SOUP

PREPARATION TIME 30 MINUTES PLUS COOLING TIME // COOKING TIME 1½ HOURS
SERVES 6

1 x 1.6 kg (3 lb 8 oz) chicken
    (preferably free-range)
15 g (½ oz) piece of ginger,
    peeled and chopped
3 garlic cloves, chopped
½ bunch coriander (cilantro),
    stems and roots roughly
    chopped, leaves reserved
    to serve
5 spring onions (scallions),
    2 left whole and the others
    sliced to serve
375 ml (13 fl oz/1½ cups) Chinese
    cooking wine
125 ml (4 fl oz/½ cup) light
    soy sauce
2 cinnamon sticks
4 star anise
270 g (9½ oz) Japanese somen
    noodles (see below)

JAPANESE SOMEN NOODLES
CAN BE FOUND IN THE ASIAN
SECTION IN SUPERMARKETS
AND AT ASIAN FOOD SHOPS.

1. Rinse the chicken and pat dry with paper towel. Put the chicken, breast side down, into your biggest saucepan and add 2 litres (70 fl oz) of water or enough to just cover. Add the ginger, garlic, coriander stems and roots, the 2 whole spring onions and the remaining ingredients, except the noodles. Bring to the boil over high heat, then reduce the heat to a simmer and cook for 1¼ hours or until the chicken is cooked, skimming any scum from the surface regularly. It should be a very gentle simmer — just the odd bubble.

2. Remove the chicken with tongs, reserving the cooking liquid. Allow the chicken to cool enough to handle.

3. Meanwhile, bring a large saucepan of water to the boil and cook the noodles according to the packet directions, then drain and refresh in cold water.

4. Coarsely shred the chicken meat from the carcass. Discard the skin and bones. Strain the reserved liquid and discard the solids.

5. Divide the noodles and chicken meat among bowls, ladle in the broth. Scatter over the sliced spring onion and coriander leaves to serve.

This is a vegetarian curry but, if you are a devoted carnivore, you could easily toss in some cubed chicken thigh just before you add the vegetables. You could also replace the pumpkin and chickpeas with other veggies. It's really important to fry the onion and spices over a low heat for a long time. Don't be tempted to whack up the heat otherwise the spices won't toast properly and the resulting curry will lack flavour and taste raw.

INDIAN PUMPKIN & CHICKPEA CURRY

PREPARATION TIME 25 MINUTES // COOKING TIME 40 MINUTES // SERVES 4

1. Heat the oil in your largest saucepan over medium–low heat and gently cook the onion, garam masala and curry powder, stirring frequently, for about 5 minutes. Add the garlic, ginger and salt and gently cook, stirring, for a further 5 minutes or until the garlic and ginger are soft. If the mixture starts to catch or burn, add a little more oil.
2. Add the tomatoes, increase the heat and boil for 5 minutes or until the liquid reduces.
3. Add the pumpkin and 250 ml (9 fl oz/1 cup) of water. Cover with a lid and simmer, stirring occasionally, for 20 minutes or until the vegetables are nearly cooked. Add the chickpeas and coconut milk and simmer until the veggies are cooked to your liking.
4. Serve the curry scattered with the coriander with the rice, yoghurt, pappadums and naan.

2 tablespoons vegetable oil
1 brown onion, diced
1½ tablespoons garam masala (see below)
1½ tablespoons curry powder
3 garlic cloves, finely chopped
25 g (1 oz) piece of ginger, peeled and finely chopped
½ teaspoon salt
400 g (14 oz) tin chopped tomatoes
600 g (1 lb 5 oz) butternut pumpkin (winter squash), peeled and diced
400 g (14 oz) tin chickpeas, drained and rinsed
400 ml (14 fl oz) coconut milk
½ cup coriander (cilantro) leaves
cooked rice (see page 31), to serve
Greek yoghurt, pappadums and naan bread, to serve (optional)

GARAM MASALA IS AN INDIAN SPICE MIX AVAILABLE AT MOST SUPERMARKETS.

IT'S BURRITO TIME!

Choose one of the fillings on the following pages, then choose a salsa, or if you are having a few mates around, consider making all of it! Also make sure you acquire some tortillas, and perhaps some freshly grated parmesan or cheddar cheese — it's not all that traditional, but it's darn tasty. Sour cream isn't bad to have on hand either if it tickles your fancy. The nine-hour braise is my favourite, but if you don't have all day to cook the meat, then the chicken with spicy tomato sauce or braised kidney beans are delicious alternatives!

TO SERVE
your choice of fillings (see pages 96–97)
your choice of salsas (see pages 100–101)
16 large corn or flour tortillas
150 g (5½ oz) finely grated parmesan or cheddar cheese
300 g (10½ oz) sour cream

SERVES 8

NINE-HOUR BURRITO BRAISE

PREPARATION TIME 30 MINUTES // COOKING TIME 9 HOURS // SERVES 8

80 ml (2½ fl oz/⅓ cup) olive oil
1.5 kg (3 lb 5 oz) boneless lamb
    shoulder, excess fat trimmed,
    cut into 3 large chunks
2 tablespoons plain (all-purpose)
    flour, for dusting
1 brown onion, roughly diced
3 garlic cloves, roughly chopped
½ red capsicum (pepper),
    seeds removed and diced
1 tablespoon ground cumin
1 tablespoon ground coriander
1 tablespoon sweet paprika
½ teaspoon cayenne pepper
80 ml (2½ fl oz/⅓ cup) red wine
400 g (14 oz) tin chopped
    tomatoes
500 ml (17 fl oz/2 cups) low-salt
    beef stock

> IF YOU HAVE A SLOW
> COOKER, YOU CAN
> TRANSFER THE MEAT AND
> BRAISING MIXTURE TO
> THAT INSTEAD OF COOKING
> IT IN THE OVEN. IF YOU
> PUT THE MEAT ON TO COOK
> ON LOW IN THE MORNING,
> IT WILL BE INCREDIBLY
> TENDER BY DINNERTIME
> AND YOUR WHOLE KITCHEN
> WILL SMELL GREAT.

1. Preheat the oven to 110°C (225°F/Gas ½). Heat the oil in a heavy-based casserole dish or an ovenproof saucepan with a tight-fitting lid over medium–high heat. Dust the lamb pieces with flour and season with salt. Cook for 2–3 minutes each side or until a deep golden brown. Remove from the pan and set aside.

2. Reduce the heat to medium, add the onion to the dish and cook, stirring, for 5 minutes or until lightly golden. Add the garlic, capsicum and spices and cook, stirring, for 2 minutes or until the garlic is starting to turn golden.

3. Pour in the red wine and once it has reduced by half, add the tomatoes. Stir, then add the lamb back to the dish. Add just enough stock to cover (top up with a little water if necessary). Bring to a simmer, then cover with a lid and cook in the oven (see left) for 8 hours or until the lamb can easily be pulled apart with a fork. (You can cool, then refrigerate the lamb in the braising liquid at this stage until you want to eat it.)

4. Remove the lamb pieces and pull apart with two forks. Discard the bones and add the meat back to the dish. Return the dish to the stovetop and simmer for 45 minutes or until the liquid has almost all evaporated (if it's too saucy, it will make the tortillas soggy). Most of the oil will be floating on the surface as it simmers, so use a wide, shallow spoon to skim off the oily layer from time to time and discard. Leave a small bowl next to the dish to put the skimmed oil into. Serve the burrito braise with the salsas.

This is an awesome go-to meal as it uses tinned tomatoes and beans, which are good to keep in your pantry to make a last-minute dinner. This braise makes the best nachos: simply heat under the grill (broiler) with some corn chips and cheese and, while the cheese is melting, chop up an avocado and a couple of spring onions (scallions) to garnish.

KIDNEY BEAN BRAISE

PREPARATION TIME 15 MINUTES // COOKING TIME 20 MINUTES // SERVES 8

1. Heat the oil in a large heavy-based saucepan over medium heat, add the onion and cook for 5 minutes, stirring, or until lightly golden. Add the garlic, capsicum, chilli and spices and cook, stirring, for 2 minutes or until dry looking.
2. Pour in the red wine and once it has reduced by half, add the tomatoes and cook for 10 minutes or until all the excess liquid has reduced.
3. Add the kidney beans, stir to combine and remove from the heat. Keep warm until serving.

80 ml (2½ fl oz/⅓ cup) olive oil
2 brown onions, finely diced
4 garlic cloves, thinly sliced
2 red capsicum (peppers),
    seeds removed and diced
4 long red chillies, sliced
1 tablespoon ground cumin
1 tablespoon ground coriander
1 tablespoon sweet paprika
125 ml (4 fl oz/½ cup) red wine
2 x 400 g (14 oz) tins
    chopped tomatoes
3 x 400 g (14 oz) tins kidney
    beans, drained and rinsed

SPICE-RUBBED CHICKEN

PREPARATION TIME 10 MINUTES // COOKING TIME 5 MINUTES // SERVES 8

1. Combine all the spices and salt and rub over the chicken pieces.
2. Heat two large frying pans, each with half of the oil, over high heat. Add half of the chicken to each pan and cook, turning occasionally, until golden brown and just cooked through.

2 teaspoons ground cumin
2 teaspoons ground coriander
2 teaspoons sweet paprika
½ teaspoon salt
1.2 kg (2 lb 10 oz) chicken thigh
    fillets, cut into 1 cm (½ inch)
    thick strips
80 ml (2½ fl oz/⅓ cup) olive oil

Clockwise from centre: Corn and coriander salsa page 100, Spice rubbed chicken page 97, Spicy tomato sauce page 101, Tomato and avocado salsa page 100, Kidney bean braise page 97, Nine-hour burrito braise page 96

SALSAS

CORN & CORIANDER SALSA

PREPARATION TIME 15 MINUTES // COOKING TIME 20 MINUTES // SERVES 8

2 cobs corn, husks intact
1 red onion
1 cup coriander (cilantro) leaves
2 long red chillies
2 tablespoons lime juice
2 tablespoons olive oil
½ teaspoon sea salt

1. Heat a large frying pan over medium heat. Put the whole corn cobs into the dry pan. Cook, turning occasionally, until the green husks have turned brown, about 20 minutes.

2. Meanwhile, finely dice the onion and chuck in a bowl with the coriander. Cut the chillies in half and scrape out the seeds if you're not a chilli lover. Thinly slice and add to the bowl.

3. Take the corn from the pan and, when cool enough to handle, carefully peel back the husks to reveal the kernels inside. Be careful of the escaping steam. Throw away the husks. Use a knife to cut off the kernels in a long, smooth cutting motion. Add to the onion mixture. Just prior to serving, add the lime juice, oil and salt and gently toss to combine.

TOMATO & AVOCADO SALSA

PREPARATION TIME 10 MINUTES // COOKING TIME NIL // SERVES 8

4 roma (plum) tomatoes,
   halved lengthways
2 Lebanese (short) cucumbers,
   peeled and halved lengthways
2 avocados, halved, stones removed,
   flesh scooped out and diced
3 spring onions (scallions), sliced
2 tablespoons lime juice
2 tablespoons olive oil
½ teaspoon sea salt

1. Use a spoon to scrape out the seeds from the tomato and cucumber and discard.

2. Dice the tomato and cucumber and combine with the avocado and spring onion. Add the lime juice, oil and salt and fold together gently with a spatula until just coated. Serve immediately.

SPICY TOMATO SAUCE

PREPARATION TIME 15 MINUTES // COOKING TIME 25 MINUTES // SERVES 8

1. Heat the oil in a heavy-based saucepan over medium heat, add the onion and cook for 5 minutes or until lightly golden. Add the garlic, capsicum and chilli and cook for 2–3 minutes or until softened. Add all the spices and salt and cook, stirring, for 1 minute or until fragrant.

2. Add the tomatoes and 185 ml (6 fl oz/¾ cup) of water and simmer for 10–15 minutes or until most of the liquid has evaporated and the sauce looks thick. Stir occasionally.

3. Taste the sauce, add more cayenne pepper if you are trying to test your friends' chilli threshold. If you're feeling fancy, you can transfer the sauce to a blender and purée until smooth. If you can't be bothered washing a blender (as I often can't!), just serve the sauce chunky. Keep warm until ready to serve.

60 ml (2 fl oz/¼ cup) olive oil
1 brown onion, finely diced
3 garlic cloves, chopped
½ red capsicum (pepper),
   seeds removed and
   finely diced
2 long red chillies, thinly sliced
2 teaspoons sweer paprika
2 teaspoons ground cumin
2 teaspoons ground coriander
¼ teaspoon cayenne pepper
½ teaspoon salt
400 g (14 oz) tin chopped
   tomatoes

HOW TO MAKE PIZZA

I know making your own pizza isn't always the most appealing idea when one can be delivered to your door with a two-minute phone conversation. But let's be honest, the pizzas are greasy, heavy, and my speculation is that the 'ham' contains at least 30 per cent possum. If you don't have time to make the base, buying one is fine — just add your own toppings. There's no right or wrong with toppings, buy try not to overload the bases too much, or the pizza will be soggy instead of crispy. I have included a few ideas to inspire.

PIZZA DOUGH

PREPARATION TIME 15 MINUTES PLUS 30 MINUTES RISING // COOKING TIME NIL
MAKES THREE 20 CM (8 INCH) PIZZA BASES

1 sachet (7 g) dried active yeast
¼ teaspoon salt
½ teaspoon caster (superfine) sugar
225 g (8 oz/1½ cups) plain (all-purpose) flour
1½ tablespoons extra virgin olive oil

1. Combine the yeast, salt, sugar and 135 ml (4½ fl oz) of lukewarm water in a small jug or bowl. Place the flour in a large bowl and make a well. Add the yeast mixture and oil.

2. Use a set of electric beaters fitted with dough hooks on medium–low speed (or an electric stand mixer) to bring the mixture together and knead for 5 minutes or until smooth and elastic. (Alternatively, mix the liquid into the flour with a wooden spoon, then knead by hand for 8 minutes.)

3. Transfer the dough to a lightly oiled bowl, cover with a tea towel and set aside in a warm place for 30 minutes or until doubled in size.

4. Use your fist to give the dough one decent punch, then divide into three portions. Roll each portion out to make a 20 cm (8 inch) round base. Transfer each to a pizza stone or a pizza tray. They are now ready to top with your favourite toppings (see pages 103–107).

MEDITERRANEAN VEGETABLES WITH HUMMUS PIZZA

PREPARATION TIME 20 MINUTES // COOKING TIME 10 MINUTES // MAKES 1

1. Preheat the oven to 210°C (415°F/Gas 6–7).
2. For the hummus base, combine all the ingredients, except the oil, in a food processor and blend for a few seconds. Stop, scrape down the side with a spatula, then blend again. While the machine is running, slowly pour in the oil until a smooth paste forms. You probably won't need all the hummus but any excess will keep in the fridge for up to 7 days.
3. Spread the hummus over the pizza base. Slice the zucchini as thin as you can using a knife or vegetable peeler. Top the pizza with the zucchini, olives, capsicum and eggplant, and crumble over the feta.
4. Bake for 10 minutes or until the base is cooked through and crispy.

1 x 20 cm (8 inch) pizza base (see opposite)
1 zucchini (courgette)
40 g (1½ oz/¼ cup) pitted Kalamata olives
120 g (4¼ oz) marinated capsicum (pepper), sliced
100 g (3½ oz) marinated eggplant (aubergine), sliced
100 g (3½ oz) feta cheese

HUMMUS
400 g (14 oz) tin chickpeas, drained and rinsed
2 garlic cloves
1 tablespoon ground cumin
1 tablespoon tahini (sesame seed paste) (optional)
finely grated zest and juice of 1 lemon
½ teaspoon salt
125 ml (4 fl oz/½ cup) olive oil

Clockwise from left:
Caramelised onion and
goat's cheese pizza page 106,
Mediterranean vegetables with
hummus pizza page 103,
Three pigs pizza page 107

CARAMELISED ONION & GOAT'S CHEESE PIZZA

PREPARATION TIME 15 MINUTES // COOKING TIME 25 MINUTES // MAKES 1

1. Preheat the oven to 210°C (415°F/Gas 6–7).
2. Heat the oil in a saucepan over medium–low heat, add the onion and a pinch of salt. Cook, stirring occasionally, for 10 minutes or until golden. Add the balsamic vinegar and sugar, reduce the heat and continue to cook until the sugar dissolves. Remove from the heat.
3. Brush the pizza base with a little olive oil, top with the onion mixture and thyme leaves. Distribute the goat's cheese in little chunks around the pizza.
4. Bake for 10 minutes or until the base is cooked through and crispy.

2 tablespoons olive oil, plus extra for brushing
2 brown onions, thinly sliced
2 teaspoons balsamic vinegar
1 teaspoon caster (superfine) sugar
1 x 20 cm (8 inch) pizza base (see page 102)
½ teaspoon thyme leaves
60 g (2¼ oz) goat's cheese

By calling this pizza three pigs, I'm claiming salami is pork,
which is not always the case. Anyhow, I digress ...

THREE PIGS PIZZA

PREPARATION TIME 15 MINUTES // COOKING TIME 20 MINUTES // MAKES 1

1. Preheat the oven to 210°C (415°F/Gas 6–7).
2. For the tomato base, pick the basil leaves and reserve ¼ cup to garnish (save left-over leaves for another pizza or other use). Thinly slice any nice-looking basil stems. Heat a frying pan over high heat, add the oil, basil stems and garlic and cook for 15 seconds or until the garlic turns translucent. Add the tomatoes and cook, stirring, for 5–10 minutes or until the watery liquid has evaporated and the sauce thickens. Season with salt and pepper. Cool slightly before using. This is enough tomato base for three pizzas. Left-over sauce will keep in the fridge in an airtight container for 3–4 days.
3. Spread the tomato base over the pizza base and scatter over the cheese. Tear the three types of meats into chunks and scatter over the pizza.
4. Bake for 10 minutes or until the base is cooked through and crispy.
5. Scatter over the reserved basil leaves and drizzle with a little oil to serve.

1 x 20 cm (8 inch) pizza base
(see page 102)
35 g (1¼ oz/¼ cup) grated
mozzarella cheese
1 bacon rasher, rind removed
2 thin prosciutto slices
5 thin salami slices
olive oil, for drizzling

TOMATO BASE
½ bunch basil
2 tablespoons olive oil
2 garlic cloves, chopped
400 g (14 oz) tinned chopped
tomatoes

IF PASSIONFRUIT AREN'T IN SEASON,
THE CURD TASTES JUST AS GOOD IF YOU
SUBSTITUTE AN EQUAL AMOUNT OF EITHER
STRAINED LEMON, ORANGE OR LIME JUICE.

PASSIONFRUIT MERINGUE TARTLETS

PREPARATION TIME 25 MINUTES // COOKING TIME 10 MINUTES // MAKES 48

1. For the passionfruit curd, bring the butter and passionfruit pulp to the boil together in a small saucepan over medium–high heat. In a bowl, whisk together the eggs and sugar until combined. Pour the boiling butter and passionfruit mixutre onto the egg mixture, whisking quickly to combine.
2. Return to the pan and cook over low heat, whisking constantly, until thickened. Remove from the heat. Whisk for a further minute or so to cool quickly, then refrigerate until cold. (You can do up to this step up to 2 days in advance.) When ready, spoon the curd into the tartlet cases and level the tops.
3. Next, make the meringue. Preheat the grill (broiler) to medium–high with the top shelf one-third of the way down. (Alternatively, use a kitchen blowtorch.) In a clean, dry bowl, use electric beaters to whisk the egg whites to firm peaks. While still beating, slowly add the sugar and beat until a stiff, shiny and dry-looking meringue forms.
4. Transfer the meringue into a piping (icing) bag fitted with a 5 mm (¼ inch) nozzle. Pipe a small amount of meringue on top of each tartlet, pulling the piping bag up to make a peak. Transfer to a baking tray and grill for 1 minute or until lightly golden (or use the blowtorch). Watch them closely because the meringue burns easily. Serve immediately.

48 x 3 cm (1¼ inch) store-bought
    shortcrust pastry tartlet cases

PASSIONFRUIT CURD
100 g (3½ oz) unsalted butter
4 passionfruit, pulp removed
    to get ⅓ cup (see note
    opposite)
3 eggs
75 g (2⅔ oz/⅓ cup) caster
    (superfine) sugar

MERINGUE
2 egg whites
75 g (2⅔ oz/⅓ cup) caster
    (superfine) sugar

FLOURLESS ORANGE & POPPY SEED CAKES WITH CARDAMOM YOGHURT

PREPARATION TIME 20 MINUTES // COOKING TIME 1 HOUR 35 MINUTES // MAKES 12

1 navel orange

2 eggs

1 egg yolk

110 g (3¾ oz/½ cup) caster
   (superfine) sugar

125 g (4½ oz/1¼ cups) almond
   meal (ground almonds)

½ teaspoon baking powder

2 teaspoons poppy seeds

CARDAMOM YOGHURT

260 g (9¼ oz/1 cup) Greek yoghurt

60 g (2¼ oz/¼ cup firmly packed)
   soft brown sugar

¼ teaspoon ground cardamom

1. Place the whole orange in a large saucepan of water, bring to the boil, then simmer for about 1¼ hours or until tender. You may need to top up the pan with water to make sure the orange remains covered.

2. Preheat the oven to 180°C (350°F/Gas 4). Grease a 12-hole, 80 ml (2½ fl oz/⅓ cup) capacity muffin tin with oil spray.

3. Cut the orange into quarters and remove any seeds. Purée the orange and the skin in a food processor until smooth.

4. Beat the eggs and yolk using an electric mixer or electric beaters for 5 minutes or until fluffy and tripled in volume. Mix in the orange purée.

5. Mix the sugar, almond meal, baking powder and poppy seeds together in a separate bowl, then fold into the egg mixture. Divide the mixture between the muffin holes. Bake for 20 minutes or until an inserted skewer comes out clean.

6. Allow to cool in the tin for 5 minutes, then run a butter knife around the edges to release the cakes and turn out.

7. For the cardamom yoghurt, combine the ingredients in a bowl and mix to create swirls.

8. Serve the cakes with the cardamom yoghurt.

FOR A MIXED BERRY ETON
MESS, OMIT THE MANGO AND
PASSIONFRUIT AND REPLACE
WITH 1 CUP OF FRESH
BERRIES. MAKE A RASPBERRY
SAUCE BY PURÉEING 125 G
(4½ OZ/1 CUP) THAWED
FROZEN RASPBERRIES, THEN
PASSING THE MIXTURE
THROUGH A FINE SIEVE.
SWIRL THE SAUCE THROUGH
THE ETON MESS.

They say that this was invented when a dog sat on a pavlova at a picnic. Rest assured you can make your own version without the aid of a dog! You can use good-quality bought meringues if you don't have time to make your own.

PASSIONFRUIT, MANGO & BLUEBERRY ETON MESS

PREPARATION TIME 30 MINUTES // COOKING TIME 1 HOUR PLUS 1 HOUR COOLING

SERVES 4

1. For the meringues, preheat the oven to 100°C (200°F/Gas ½) non fan-forced and line a baking tray with baking paper.
2. Using electric beaters, whisk the egg white until soft peaks start to form. While beating, slowly add the sugar and beat until very stiff peaks form. Spoon or pipe about ⅓ cupfuls of the mixture onto the lined tray, leaving space in between each for spreading. Bake for 1 hour. Turn off the oven, prop open the door slightly with a wooden spoon and leave to cool for 1 hour before removing.
3. Combine the cream, icing sugar and vanilla bean paste and whisk to soft peaks.
4. To serve, crumble the meringues into bite-sized pieces. Combine the meringue pieces with the cream mixture. Fold through the mango, passionfruit pulp and blueberries. Don't overmix to ensure you get swirls of yellow passionfruit going through the white cream mixture. Divide among small glasses and serve immediately.

300 ml (10½ fl oz) thickened (whipping) cream
2 tablespoons icing (confectioner's) sugar, sifted
1 teaspoon vanilla bean paste
1 mango, flesh sliced
4 passionfruit, pulp scooped out or 170 g (6 oz) tin pulp
150 g (5½ oz) fresh blueberries

MERINGUES
2 egg whites
80 g (2¾ oz) caster (superfine) sugar
½ teaspoon cornflour (cornstarch)
½ teaspoon white vinegar

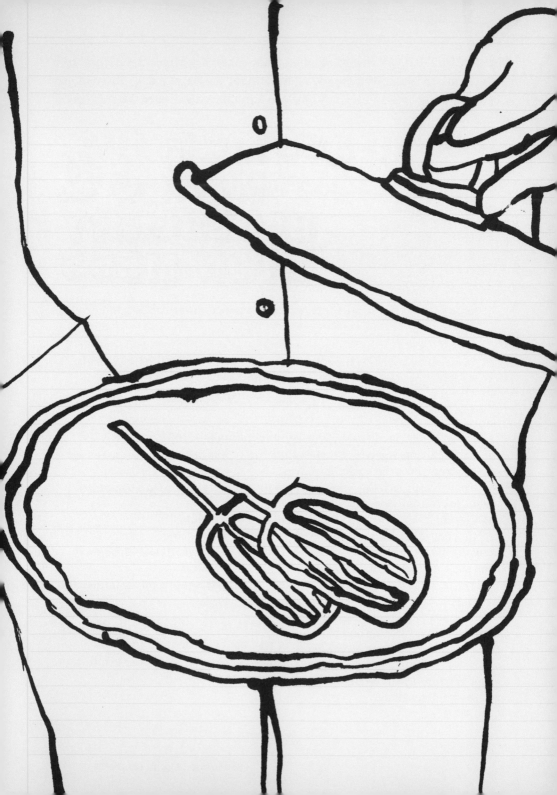

SOMETHING SPECIAL

I have probably proclaimed my love for eating quite a few times in this book already, but it is the entire reason I became interested in cooking in the first place! I thought if I could learn to cook well I could continue to eat well, and so when I moved out of home I could hopefully avoid consuming several tonnes of two-minute noodles. (Actually, I had a lecturer at uni who was bald and he blamed it on the MSG in the noodles he ate every day while he was studying!)

But what about my love of preparing food? I have come to love the whole process, not just the finished result. (I'm a firm believer that a cake batter will taste better than the cake 100 per cent of the time.) These recipes are some of my favourites when I'm cooking for fun, not just dinner. Food can often take a while to prepare and can be gobbled up in minutes, so you might as well enjoy the preparation. These dishes are great for impressing the people you are feeding, or better yet get them in the kitchen to give you a hand. Some of my first memories are being in the kitchen, 'helping' to make a cake, most of which involved getting in the way and licking the beaters.

This dish was a collaborative effort between myself and my mate Matt who showed me a thing or two about using a wok. My wok doesn't have a lid, and you really need one to steam mussels open properly. Matt rinsed out the big metal bowl we had the mussels in, flipped it upside down and put it over the wok. Best lid I've ever seen! Don't be a goose like I was and try to use your hands to get the bowl off — tongs or a tea towel are much safer options!

CHILLI JAM MUSSELS STEAMED WITH BEER

PREPARATION TIME 25 MINUTES // COOKING TIME 10 MINUTES
SERVES 2 AS A MAIN OR 4 AS PART OF A SHARED MEAL OR BANQUET

1 kg (2 lb 4 oz) mussels
170 ml (5½ fl oz/⅔ cup)
   Asahi beer
¼ cup coriander (cilantro) leaves
lime cheeks and crusty bread,
   to serve

CHILLI BASE
2 tablespoons peanut oil
4 long red chillies, seeds removed
   and cut into a couple of pieces
2 red Asian shallots, cut into
   a couple of pieces
4 garlic cloves
20 g (¾ oz) piece of ginger, peeled
   and roughly chopped
1 teaspoon shrimp paste, toasted
   (optional) (see opposite)
1 bunch coriander (cilantro), stems
   and roots only, washed
2 teaspoons chopped palm sugar
   (jaggery)
2 teaspoons light soy sauce

1. If there is any excess stuff growing on your mussels, scrub them in water. 'Debeard' your mussels by pulling the little beards that are present at the seam of the mussel up and out. (Scrubbed and debearded mussels are available from seafood shops. They're also called pot-ready mussels.) Set aside.

2. For the chilli base, blend the oil, chilli, shallot, garlic, ginger, shrimp paste, and coriander roots and stems in a food processor until finely chopped.

3. Heat a wok over high heat, add the chilli base and cook, stirring, for 2 minutes or until fragrant. Add the palm sugar and soy sauce and stir until the sugar dissolves.

4. Add the beer and, when it comes to the boil, add the mussels. Cover with a lid or an upside down metal bowl and steam, shaking the wok occasionally, for 2–5 minutes or until the mussels open. Remove the mussels from the wok as they open so they don't overcook. Once they have all opened, return them to the wok.

5. Scatter with the coriander and serve with lime cheeks, bread and perhaps another beer!

SHRIMP PASTE STINKS TO HIGH
HEAVEN, BUT ADDS AMAZING
DEPTH AND COMPLEXITY TO
FOOD. IT'S AVAILABLE FROM
ASIAN FOOD SHOPS. TO TOAST,
ADD TO A FRYING PAN OVER
MEDIUM HEAT AND COOK UNTIL
IT IS DRY AND AROMATIC.

MUSHROOM & GOAT'S CHEESE RISOTTO

PREPARATION TIME 25 MINUTES // COOKING TIME 30 MINUTES // SERVES 2

1. Heat 1 tablespoon of the oil in a medium to large heavy-based saucepan over medium heat, add the onion and cook gently, stirring occasionally with a wooden spoon, for 10 minutes or until translucent. Increase to medium–high heat, add the garlic and cook for 1 minute, then add the rice. Cook, stirring for a further minute to toast the rice.

2. Add half the butter, stir to coat, then add the wine. Once the wine bubbles away, add the porcini mushroom soaking water, then add the hot stock, a ladleful at a time, waiting for each addition to be absorbed before adding the next. This process will take 16–18 minutes. Stir occasionally. If you run out of stock and the rice needs a little more cooking, use hot water or more stock.

3. While the risotto is cooking, heat 2 teaspoons of the remaining oil in a large frying pan over medium–high heat. Add half the mixed mushrooms and a pinch of salt and cook until golden. Remove from the pan and repeat with the remaining oil and mushrooms. Return all the mushrooms to the pan, along with the porcini mushrooms and season with salt. Stir in the thyme and remaining butter. Reduce the heat to low and cook gently until the rice is al dente (soft but still with a little bite).

4. Stir in the pecorino and most of the parsley. Divide among bowls, top with the mushroom mixture, scatter with the remaining parsley and top with the goat's cheese.

2 tablespoons olive oil

½ brown onion, finely diced

2 garlic cloves, chopped

140 g (5 oz/⅔ cup) arborio rice

30 g (1 oz) butter

60 ml (2 fl oz/¼ cup) white wine

10 g (⅓ oz) dried porcini mushrooms, soaked in 60 ml (2 fl oz/¼ cup) hot water, drained and soaking water reserved

500 ml (17 fl oz/2 cups) low-salt chicken or vegetable stock, heated with 125 ml (4 fl oz/½ cup) water in a saucepan until boiling, then kept warm

250 g (9 oz) mixed mushrooms, cut into pieces (try to get a mixture, such as field, button, shiitake, king brown and oyster)

3 thyme or lemon thyme sprigs, leaves picked

25 g (1 oz) grated pecorino cheese (or parmesan)

¼ cup flat-leaf (Italian) parsley leaves, chopped

50 g (1¾ oz) goat's cheese

SPICED LAMB WITH POMEGRANATE COUSCOUS & HONEY YOGHURT DRESSING

PREPARATION TIME 20 MINUTES // COOKING TIME 15 MINUTES // SERVES 2

2 tablespoons vegetable
or olive oil
2 teaspoons ground cumin
2 teaspoons ground coriander
½ teaspoon salt
6 lamb cutlets or 400 g (14 oz)
lamb backstraps
1 teaspoon tahini (sesame
seed paste) (optional)
1 quantity honey–yoghurt dressing
(see page 156)
2 tablespoons pomegranate
molasses (see below),
to serve (optional)

POMEGRANATE COUSCOUS
100 g (3½ oz) instant couscous
2 teaspoons olive oil
125 ml (4 fl oz/½ cup) chicken
stock
½ cup mint leaves
½ pomegranate, seeds removed
35 g (1¼ oz/¼ cup) slivered
almonds
2 tablespoons dates or raisins,
chopped

1. Combine half of the oil, the cumin, coriander and salt together in a bowl and rub into the lamb.

2. Stir the tahini into the honey–yoghurt dressing.

3. For the pomegranate couscous, place the couscous in a heatproof bowl and rub in the oil. Bring the stock to the boil and pour over the couscous. Leave for 1 minute, then fluff with a fork. Leave to sit for 10 minutes, fluffing occasionally until there are no lumps. When cool, stir through the pomegranate seeds, almonds and dates.

4. Heat the remaining oil in a large frying pan over medium–high heat. Add the lamb and cook for 3–4 minutes or until a deep golden brown all over.

5. Serve the lamb drizzled with the pomegranate molasses, honey–yoghurt dressing and the couscous on the side.

POMEGRANATE MOLASSES
CAN BE FOUND IN DELIS AND
MIDDLE EASTERN GROCERS.

A duck spends a good chunk of its life in the water, and so they have a thick layer of fat covering their breasts to keep them warm. This isn't very enjoyable to eat, so it's important to render out that fat over low heat before crisping up the skin. It's quite surprising when you put the duck into a cold pan and bring up the heat just how much fat comes out. Don't waste this fat (duck fat costs about $12 for a small tub) — I pour it into a little container and use it to make the most delicious roast vegetables. The duck is rich and tender, so it's great served with a crunchy salad or stir-fried greens and noodles.

FIVE-SPICE HONEY DUCK

PREPARATION TIME 5 MINUTES // COOKING TIME 10 MINUTES // SERVES 2

1. Preheat the oven to 180°C (350°F/Gas 4) Lightly score the duck skin, being careful not to cut through to the flesh. Season the skin with salt. Combine the honey and five-spice in a small bowl and set aside.

2. Place the duck, skin side down, in a cold ovenproof frying pan and season the flesh with salt. Place the duck over medium heat and allow the fat to slowly render out. This will take a few minutes. Increase the heat and, once the skin is a deep golden brown, turn over, discarding all but 1 tablespoon of fat in the pan. Brush the duck skin with the honey mixture, then put the pan in the oven for 5 minutes or until the duck is cooked to your liking.

3. Allow the duck to rest for a couple of minutes before thinly slicing and serving.

2 duck breasts (about 250 g/9 oz each)
1 tablespoon honey
1 teaspoon Chinese five-spice

CRISPY SKIN SALMON WITH THAI SALAD & CHILLI CARAMEL

PREPARATION TIME 40 MINUTES // COOKING TIME 20 MINUTES // SERVES 4

4 x 200 g (7 oz) salmon fillets,
    pin-boned and skin scraped
    clean of scales with a knife
2 tablespoons vegetable oil
cooked rice (see page 31), to serve

CHILLI CARAMEL
70 g (2½ oz/½ cup) roughly
    chopped or grated light palm
    sugar (jaggery) (see opposite)
1 long red chilli, thinly sliced
1 tablespoon fish sauce
1½ tablespoons lime juice

SALAD
1 long red chilli, seeds removed
    and thinly sliced
4 spring onions (scallions), thinly
    sliced on an angle
50 g (1¾ oz/⅓ cup) roasted
    peanuts
115 g (4 oz/1 cup) bean sprouts
1 cup coriander (cilantro) leaves
1 cup mint leaves
250 g (9 oz) cherry tomatoes, halved
1 quantity Thai dressing
    (see page 156)

1. Preheat the oven to 200°C (400°F/Gas 6).
2. For the chilli caramel, place the palm sugar and 125 ml (4 fl oz/½ cup) of water in a heavy-based saucepan and heat gently, stirring, to dissolve the sugar. Bring to the boil, reduce the heat and simmer for 5–8 minutes or until a light caramel forms. Once simmering, don't stir; instead brush down the sides of the pan with a wet pastry brush from time to time.
3. Once the caramel darkens slightly, remove from heat and add 1 tablespoon of water, being careful as it may spit. Add the chilli and leave to cool. Stir in the fish sauce and lime juice, then taste and adjust — you want a balance of sweet, salty, sour and hot.
4. For the salad, combine all the ingredients, except the dressing, in a bowl, cover with plastic wrap and refrigerate until needed.
5. Season the salmon skin with salt. Heat the oil in a wide, ovenproof frying pan over medium–high heat. Add the salmon, skin side down, and cook for 3–4 minutes or until the skin is crisp. Check after 1–2 minutes. If the skin looks like it is starting to burn, reduce the heat. Turn the salmon over, transfer the pan to the oven and cook for 4 minutes or until cooked to your liking.
6. Dress the salad and divide among plates. Top with the salmon and drizzle with the chilli caramel. Serve with the rice.

LIGHT PALM SUGAR MEANS
LIGHT IN COLOUR AND IT CAN
BE FOUND IN SUPERMARKETS
AND ASIAN FOOD SHOPS.

This dish is inspired by Maha, a Melbourne restaurant I spent a few weeks at. I have fond memories of packing down at the end of the night. There would often be left-over pork belly and all the staff would grab a bread roll, tear it open and fill it with delicious meat to feed on. In hindsight, it probably wasn't the ideal meal to eat just before going to bed, but it is a great dish for entertaining because you can cook the pork the day before and just finish it in the pan. This will feed four people if you serve it with bread and a light entrée beforehand.

CONFIT PORK BELLY WITH CELERIAC & APPLE SLAW

PREPARATION TIME 1 HOUR PLUS CHILLING OVERNIGHT
COOKING TIME 6–8 HOURS // SERVES 4

CONFIT PORK BELLY

1 x 800 g (1 lb 12 oz) piece boneless
    pork belly, skin on
2 litres (70 fl oz) olive oil,
    plus 1 tablespoon to serve
3 cinnamon sticks
3 star anise
2 bay leaves
2 tablespoons pomegranate seeds,
    to serve (optional)

CELERIAC AND APPLE SLAW

2 granny smith (green) apples, cut into
    thin matchsticks
220 g (7 ¾ oz) peeled celeriac (celery root)
    (see opposite), cut into thin matchsticks
    or coarsely grated
1 tablespoon flat-leaf (Italian) parsley
    leaves, torn
60 g (2¼ oz/½ cup) walnuts,
    very roughly chopped
2 tablespoons good-quality mayonnaise
2 teaspoons olive oil
2 teaspoons lemon juice

> CELERIAC IS A WINTER ROOT VEGETABLE THAT
> IS ROUGH, KNOBBLY AND ABOUT THE SIZE
> OF A GRAPEFRUIT. IT HAS A MILD, SLIGHTLY
> SWEET FLAVOUR. IT'S ALSO GREAT AS A MASH.

1. Rub the pork generously with salt. In a deep flameproof roasting tray slightly larger than the pork, heat the oil on the stovetop to about 90°C (194°F). Add the pork, making sure it is completely covered by the oil. Add the cinnamon, star anise and bay leaves and cover with a piece of baking paper.
2. Preheat the oven to 110°C (225°F/Gas ½). Check the pork after 45 minutes; if it is bubbling a lot, then you will need to reduce the oven temperature to 100°C (200°F). Cook in the oven for 6–8 hours or until tender and almost falling apart.
3. Remove the pork from the oil, allow any excess oil to drip off and place, skin side down, between two baking trays wrapped in plastic wrap. Transfer the pork to the fridge and place a weight on top (use heavy food tins, a brick or pumpkin) and refrigerate overnight. Strain the oil and allow to cool completely before discarding, or save and re-use this oil next time you confit pork.
4. The next day, when ready to eat, preheat oven to 220°C (425°F/Gas 7).
5. For the celeriac and apple slaw, combine the apple, celeriac, parsley, walnuts and mayonnaise. Add the oil and lemon juice, season with salt and pepper, then taste and adjust the balance of flavours with a little more lemon juice or oil if needed.
6. Cut the pork belly into four rectangles, about 10 cm x 3 cm (4 x 1¼ inches), but this will vary depending on the shape and size of your pork belly. Season each piece with salt. Heat 1 tablespoon of oil (from cooking the pork) in a frying pan over high heat, add the pork pieces and cook on all sides except the skin, then drain all the oil from the pan. Turn over and cook, skin side down, for 3 minutes or until crisp. Turn over again, so it's skin side up, transfer to the oven and cook for 5 minutes to ensure the skin is nice and crispy.
7. Serve the pork with the slaw and scatter over a few pomegranate seeds to finish.

This is a great recipe if you either don't have an oven or simply just enjoy delicious food. It's more of a terrine than a cake, and it's basically just a matter of melting and combining all the ingredients and setting it in the fridge. It will become quite hard once it's chilled, so when you turn it out to serve, get a big knife and run some hot water over it to make cutting it easier.

NO-BAKE CHOCOLATE CAKE

PREPARATION TIME 30 MINUTES PLUS 3 HOURS CHILLING // COOKING TIME 5 MINUTES
SERVES 8

500 g (1 lb 2 oz) good-quality dark chocolate, chopped

100 g (3½ oz) unsalted butter, chopped

395 g (13¾ oz) sweetened condensed milk

200 g (7 oz) digestive biscuits

100 g (3½ oz/¾ cup) roughly chopped pistachio nuts, plus extra to serve

45 g (1⅔ oz/⅓ cup) slivered almonds

160 g (5⅔ oz) dried figs, roughly chopped (optional)

250 ml (9 fl oz/1 cup) pouring (single) cream, to serve

250 g (9 oz) crème fraîche, to serve

1. Grease and line a 20 cm x 8 cm (8 x 3¼ inch) loaf (bar) tin or terrine mould with baking paper.

2. Combine the chocolate, butter and condensed milk in a heatproof bowl. Fill a saucepan that the bowl will fit over one-third full of water and bring to the boil. Place the bowl over the saucepan and melt the ingredients together, stirring occasionally.

3. Put the biscuits in a plastic bag and tap lightly with a rolling pin or other heavy object until roughly broken.

4. In a large bowl, combine the crushed biscuits with the pistachios, almonds and figs. Pour over the hot chocolate mixture and mix well. Transfer the mixture into the tin, pushing it down to remove any air bubbles, and smooth the surface. Refrigerate for 3 hours or until firm.

5. Whisk the cream and crème fraîche together until soft peaks form. Turn out the cake, and cut into slices. Serve with a dollop of the cream mixture and some extra pistachios.

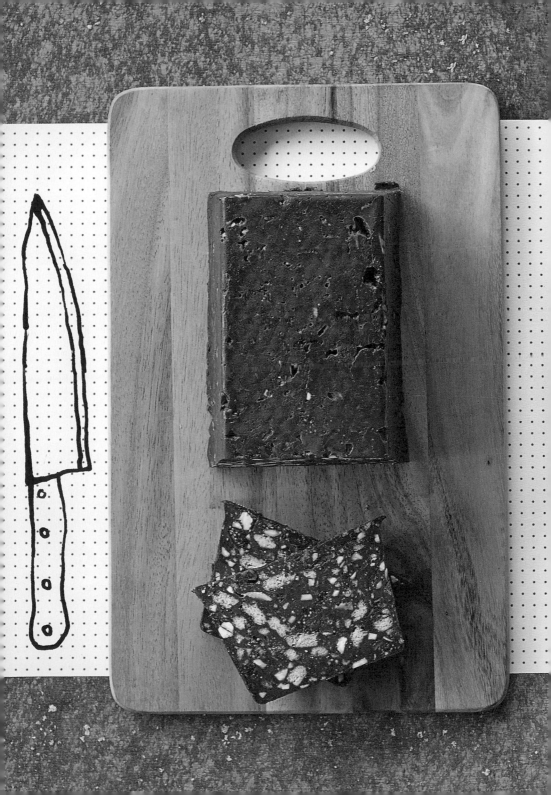

This is the first dish I remember cooking. I made it for my mum for Mother's Day and it has become a bit of a tradition in my family every year. If you have a good-quality non-stick frying pan, try my trick of using absolutely no butter or oil when cooking the pancakes — you end up with really pro-looking cakes that are the same golden colour all over.

MOTHER'S DAY PANCAKES

PREPARATION TIME 15 MINUTES // COOKING TIME 20 MINUTES // SERVES 4

1. Sift the flour and bicarbonate of soda together into a large bowl. Make a well in the centre with your fingers.
2. In a jug or bowl, whisk together the eggs, milk and sugar. Pour into the well and whisk to combine. Making the well helps to stop lumps forming in the batter.
3. Heat a non-stick frying pan over medium heat and add ¼–⅓ cup of the batter. Cook for 1–2 minutes or until lots of bubbles form on the surface, then carefully flip with a spatula and cook for a further minute. Remove from the pan and repeat with the remaining batter. Stack pancakes on top of each other while you're cooking to keep them warm.
4. Serve the pancakes with your choice of toppings.

260 g (9¼ oz/1¾ cups) self-raising flour
¼ teaspoon bicarbonate of soda (baking soda)
2 eggs
310 ml (10¾ fl oz/1¼ cups) milk
165 g (5¾ oz/¾ cup) caster (superfine) sugar

TOPPINGS
banana, ice cream and maple syrup (Mum's favourite)
fig, ricotta and honey, or strawberries and nutella (my favourites)
lemon juice and caster (superfine) sugar (my sister, Kirsty's, favourite)
plain (Chloe's favourite. My girlfriend is really weird. Who likes plain pancakes?)

I remember sticking some yoghurt in the freezer to see if it would turn into frozen yoghurt but it ended up being a big frozen block. But when I scratched it with a fork, it formed a fluffy granita that has a cool texture like snow.

BLUEBERRY FRANGIPANE LOAF WITH YOGHURT GRANITA

PREPARATION TIME 35 MINUTES PLUS 3 HOURS FREEZING
COOKING TIME 45 MINUTES // SERVES 6

YOGHURT GRANITA
500 g (1 lb 2 oz) thick unsweetened Greek yoghurt
30 g (1 oz/¼ cup) icing (confectioner's) sugar

BLUEBERRY FRANGIPANE
175 g icing (confectioner's) sugar
100 g (3½ oz/1 cup) almond meal (ground almonds)
35 g (1¼ oz) plain (all-purpose) flour
125 g (4½ oz) unsalted butter, chopped and softened
2 eggs
250 g (9 oz) fresh blueberries

1. For the yoghurt granita, stir together the yoghurt and icing sugar in a bowl. Transfer to a freezer-safe container and place in the freezer for 3 hours or until hard.

2. For the blueberry frangipane, preheat the oven to 190°C (375°F/Gas 5). Grease and line a 24 cm x 12 cm (9½ x 4½ inch) loaf (bar) tin with baking paper.

3. Sift the icing sugar, then the almond meal and flour into a large bowl. Use an electric mixer or electric beaters to beat in the butter until just combined. Beat in 1 egg and, once it has been completely combined with the other ingredients, beat in the other egg. Gently fold through half of the blueberries.

4. Spoon the mixture into the tin and level it out with a spatula. Bake for 40–45 minutes or until an inserted skewer comes out clean. Remove from the oven and cool in the tin. Carefully remove and cut into fat slices.

5. Using a fork, scratch up the surface of the granita in long, smooth strokes to form a snow-like consistency. Serve immediately with the frangipane and the remaining blueberries.

NO-SET PEACH & RASPBERRY CHEESECAKE

PREPARATION TIME 35 MINUTES // COOKING TIME 5 MINUTES // SERVES 4

8 gingernut biscuits
50 g (1¾ oz/⅓ cup) hazelnuts,
    halved
40 g (1½ oz) butter
½ quantity lemon curd (see
    passionfruit meringue
    tartlets tip on page 108)
4 yellow or white peaches,
    cut into wedges
125 g (4½ oz/1 cup) fresh
    raspberries

CHEESECAKE MOUSSE
250 g (9 oz) cream cheese, at room
    temperature
80 g (2¾ oz/¼ cup) sweetened
    condensed milk
2 tablespoons lemon juice
170 ml (5½ fl oz/⅔ cup) thickened
    (whipping) cream

1. You need to turn the biscuits into crumbs, but not a powder, so either blend in a food processor until just broken down or place in a zip-lock bag have a field day with a rolling pin or saucepan.

2. Heat a small frying pan over medium–high heat, add the hazelnuts and toast for a few minutes, tossing regularly. You'll know they're toasted when they begin to lose their skins, turn golden and start to smell strongly of nuts. When toasted, add the butter and reduce the heat to medium. When the butter has melted, add the crumbled biscuits and toss around a bit until the crumbs are coated. Transfer to a bowl to cool.

3. For the cheesecake mousse, using an electric mixer or electric beaters, beat the cream cheese until very soft. Add the condensed milk and lemon juice and beat until combined. In a separate bowl, whip the cream to firm peaks, then fold into the cream cheese mixture.

4. Divide the cheesecake mousse among bowls, add some lemon curd and hazelnut crumbs and arrange the peach and raspberries around. If you are trying to impress someone, spoon one-quarter of the hazelnut crumbs into the base of martini glasses, spoon in some lemon curd, then mousse and arrange the fruit around the rim. Serve straight away.

The best part about these cupcakes is that they can be made to suit any occasion — I make them green for St Patrick's day and pink for Valentine's.

CELEBRATION CUPCAKES

PREPARATION TIME 30 MINUTES PLUS 1 HOUR CHILLING
COOKING TIME 20 MINUTES // MAKES 24

1. For the white chocolate ganache icing, combine the white chocolate and butter in a bowl. Bring the cream and food colouring to the boil in a small saucepan and pour over the chocolate and butter. Allow to sit for a minute, then stir until smooth. Put in the fridge for 1 hour or until firm but a spreadable consistency.

2. Preheat the oven to 170°C (325°F/Gas 3). Line two 12-hole patty pan tins with paper cases. Using an electric mixer or electric beaters, beat together the sugar, eggs and butter in a large bowl until just combined, then add the flour and milk. Mix again until the mixture comes together and becomes a little pale.

3. Divide the mixture between the patty pan holes and bake for 20 minutes or until slightly golden and only a few crumbs cling to an inserted skewer. Remove from the oven and cool for 5 minutes in the tins, then lift out and cool completely on a wire rack.

4. Once the cakes have cooled to room temperature, beat the chilled ganache with electric beaters for 30 seconds or until light and fluffy, but don't beat for too long or the ganache may split. Use a smooth knife to ice the cupcakes with the ganache and top with the lollies.

220 g (7¾ oz/1 cup) caster superfine) sugar
2 eggs
90 g (3¼ oz) unsalted butter, melted
300 g (10½ oz/2 cups) self-raising flour, sifted
250 ml (9 fl oz/1 cup) milk
colourful lollies, such as jellybeans, or candy-covered chocolates, to serve (optional)

WHITE CHOCOLATE GANACHE ICING
300 g (10½ oz) white chocolate, chopped
90 g (3¼ oz) unsalted butter, chopped
180 ml (5⅔ fl oz) pouring (single) cream
a few drops of food colouring (optional)

VANILLA PANNA COTTA WITH BALSAMIC BERRIES

PREPARATION TIME 20 MINUTES PLUS 4 HOURS CHILLING
COOKING TIME 5 MINUTES // MAKES 6

600 ml (21 fl oz) thickened (whipping) cream
1 vanilla bean, split and seeds scraped (or 1 teaspoon vanilla bean paste)
100 g (3½ oz) caster (superfine) sugar
2 x gold-strength (2 g each) gelatine leaves, soaked in cold water for 5 minutes, then squeezed to remove excess water (see below)

BALSAMIC BERRIES
250 g (9 oz) fresh mixed berries, strawberries (sliced if large)
30 g (1 oz/¼ cup) icing (confectioner's) sugar
2 teaspoons balsamic vinegar

> GOLD-STRENGTH GELATINE LEAVES ARE AVAILABLE FROM SELECTED DELIS AND GROCERS.

1. Lightly grease six 125 ml (4 fl oz/½ cup) capacity plastic dariole moulds with oil spray. Combine the cream, vanilla bean and seeds and sugar in a saucepan and bring to a gentle simmer, stirring until all the sugar has dissolved. Remove from the heat and discard the vanilla bean halves. Add the gelatine leaves and stir until dissolved.

2. Transfer to a bowl over ice and stir until cooled and nearly starting to set. (You can pour the mixture into the dariole moulds while it's hot if you can't be bothered waiting, but allowing it to cool before distributing ensures all the vanilla seeds don't fall to the bottom.) Pour the mixture into the moulds and leave to set in the fridge for at least 4 hours. Pat yourself on the back for a job well done. Put on your Sunday best and prepare to woo the nearest person.

3. Half an hour or so before you plan to eat, combine all the ingredients for the balsamic berries in a bowl.

4. To remove a panna cotta from its mould, turn it on its side and use your fingers to tease it away from the edges. Once an air pocket forms, invert on a serving plate, squeeze the sides gently and it should slip out. Serve with the balsamic berries and a little of the berry syrup spooned over.

PANNA COTTA VARIATIONS

COCONUT WITH MANGO, LYCHEE & MINT SALAD

Replace half the thickened cream with coconut cream. Increase the gelatine to 2½ leaves. Cut the cheeks from 1 large mango, use a large spoon to scoop out the flesh and thinly slice. Tear some mint leaves and add to the mango, along with 200 g (7 oz) drained tinned lychees. Arrange the salad around each panna cotta. Add a few blobs of lime or lemon curd if you can be bothered to make some (see passionfruit meringue tartlets tip on page 108). Sprinkle with toasted black sesame seeds to finish.

YOGHURT WITH FIGS & HONEY

Replace half the thickened cream with good-quality natural yoghurt or sheep's milk yoghurt. Bring the cream, vanilla bean and seeds and sugar to a gentle simmer, then remove the pan from the heat. Add the softened and squeezed gelatine, stir to dissolve, then leave to cool for 2 minutes before whisking in the yoghurt. Pass the mixture through a fine-mesh sieve to get rid of any lumps. Cut a few figs into 6 pieces each and arrange 3 pieces around each panna cotta. Drizzle with honey and scatter over a few chopped pistachio nuts.

Vanilla panna cotta with balsamic berries page 134

GRAB AND GO

As much as I love eating, sometimes sitting down to a meal can be a bit of a luxury. It's good to have some dishes up your sleeve that you can take with you or that are super quick for when you are running a bit late. I'm the kind of person who is always running late to everything, so I wanted to include some of my favourite foods for eating on the go.

Some of the recipes in this chapter are five-minute jobs, which you can make before a busy day to give you the energy you need, such as the banana and ricotta toast (see page 140). The other recipes are things I like to make when I have a bit of free time and that will last me a couple of days of snacking, such as the white chocolate and pistachio biscuits (see page 149). (I wrote 'last me a couple of days of snacking' because I thought it would sound good but, in all honesty, these biscuits are addictive and it's hard not to eat them all fresh out of the oven!)

This is such a quick breakfast, I'm not even sure if it qualifies as a recipe. I wanted to include it because I can eat it on the go, even when I'm running super late.

BANANA & RICOTTA TOAST

PREPARATION TIME 5 MINUTES // COOKING TIME 3 MINUTES
SERVES 1 HUNGRY PERSON

2–3 thick slices bread (or brioche is a great alternative)
115 g (4 oz/½ cup) fresh ricotta cheese (see below)
1 banana, sliced
honey, to serve
¼ teaspoon ground cinnamon

1. Toast the bread. Spread each slice with some of the ricotta. Top with the banana, drizzle with a little honey and dust with the cinnamon.

RICOTTA IS BEST FROM THE DELI SECTION OF YOUR SUPERMARKET.

People love this when I make it for them, and then proceed to freak out when I say I put an egg in it. Eggs in drinks isn't weird though, right? Right! ... Eggnog seems pretty popular. The egg thickens the drink and makes it really rich and smooth, almost like thin chocolate custard. Don't knock it till you try it.

DON'T TELL ANYONE THERE'S AN EGG IN IT HOT CHOCOLATE

PREPARATION TIME 5 MINUTES // COOKING TIME 3 MINUTES // SERVES 1

1. Grab a small saucepan and put it over medium heat. While it heats up, beat together the egg and sugar in a heatproof bowl.
2. Add the milk, then the chocolate to the hot pan and stir constantly until the chocolate has melted. Once melted and the milk is hot, but not boiling, take off the heat and quickly whisk the chocolate mixture into the egg mixture. Once smooth, pour into a mug, top with the grated chocolate and sip away.

1 egg
1 teaspoon caster (superfine) sugar
185 ml (6 fl oz/¾ cup) milk
50 g (1¾ oz) good-quality dark chocolate (70% cocoa solids), plus extra grated, to serve

The recent thought by burger enthusiasts on a great burger is to let the beef speak for itself — seasoned with salt and nothing else. No breadcrumbs, egg, onion or any other fillers or binding agents. I like this idea of less is more. Almost think of it like a steak.

THE ULTIMATE CHEESEBURGER

PREPARATION TIME 25 MINUTES // COOKING TIME 10 MINUTES
MAKES 6 SMALL BURGERS

500 g (1 lb 2 oz) minced (ground) beef (see below)

1¼ teaspoons salt

vegetable oil, for cooking

6 thin slices cheddar cheese (about 120 g/4¼ oz in total)

60 ml (2 fl oz/¼ cup) tomato sauce (ketchup) (I like Heinz)

60 g (2¼ oz/¼ cup) Dijon or American-style mustard (optional)

4 small dill pickles, sliced

6 small soft white buns

DON'T BUY LEAN MINCED MEAT; IT NEEDS TO BE ABOUT 80% MEAT AND 20 % FAT SO IT DOESN'T DRY OUT, ASK THE BUTCHER SPECIFICALLY FOR CHUCK TO BE MINCED FOR YOU. IT'S IMPORTANT THE BUN IS WHITE — IT HAS TO BE ABOUT THE SIMPLICITY OF THE MEAT, SAUCE AND CHEESE.

1. Preheat the grill (broiler) to high.
2. Spread the minced beef over the base of a large bowl and scatter the salt evenly across it. Get your hand into the bowl and really work the mince around to make sure the salt is evenly distributed. Divide the mince into 6 portions and roll each into a ball. Heat a large frying pan with enough oil to just cover the base of the pan over medium heat. Add the patties to the pan and flatten to about 2 cm (¾ inch) thick with a spatula. Cook for about 4 minutes or until the patties have developed a deep golden brown crust.
3. Turn the patties over and reduce the heat to low. Top each with a slice of cheese and cook for a further 4 minutes or until the patties are just cooked through and the cheese has melted.
4. Cut each bun in half and stick them under the grill, cut side up, to lightly toast. Add a patty to each bun base, top with the sauce, mustard and pickles and sandwich with the tops.

This is dude food at its best, the sort of stuff you can make in about 20 minutes on the barbecue with a Corona in one hand.

DUDE FOOD CORN

PREPARATION TIME 5 MINUTES // COOKING TIME 20 MINUTES

SERVES 2–4 AS A SNACK

1. Heat a barbecue flatplate or large frying pan over high heat. Cook the cobs of corn in their husks, turning every couple of minutes, until browned and blackened all over. This will take about 15 minutes.
2. Once the corn is cooked, transfer to a big bowl and cover with plastic wrap to allow the corn to steam itself a bit.
3. Let the corn cool for a few minutes, then peel off the husks. Cut off the ends of the corn, squeeze the lime halves over the cobs, add a knob of butter and scatter over the parmesan. If you want the cheese to melt a bit more, put the cobs under a hot grill (broiler). Top with the chilli and coriander. Eat with your hands.

4 cobs corn, husks intact

2 limes, halved

50 g (1¾ oz) butter

50 g (1¾ oz/⅓ cup) finely grated parmesan cheese

1 long red chilli, seeds removed (unless you like it hot) and finely chopped

¼ cup coriander (cilantro) leaves, roughly chopped

For me this is the king of steak sandwiches, and it is really quick to make. It also gets me in the good books with my girlfriend, Chloe. I'm glad one of her favourite dishes is also one of my quickest!

CHLOE'S FAVOURITE VEAL SANDWICH

PREPARATION TIME 10 MINUTES // COOKING TIME 5 MINUTES // SERVES 2

4 thick slices ciabatta or other crusty bread

2 veal minute steaks or schnitzels (uncrumbed)

1 tablespoon olive oil

1 tablespoon Dijon mustard

60 g (2¼ oz) good-quality cheddar cheese, sliced

2 dill pickles, sliced

¼ red onion, thinly sliced

1. Preheat the grill (broiler) to high. Toast the bread until just golden on both sides.

2. Season the veal, then cook in a very hot frying pan with the olive oil for 1 minute each side or until cooked to your liking.

3. Spread the mustard onto half of the toasted bread slices. Top with the slices of cheese, place back under the grill and cook until the cheese has melted.

4. Top the melted cheese with the dill pickles, onion, a piece of veal and sandwich with the remaining toast. Cut each sandwich in half to serve.

Everyone needs a good biscuit recipe up their sleeve, and this one is a cracker. I can only assume these keep quite well in an airtight container — I don't think they have ever lasted long enough for me to test the theory!

WHITE CHOCOLATE & PISTACHIO BISCUITS

PREPARATION TIME 20 MINUTES

COOKING TIME 25 MINUTES // MAKES 26

1. Preheat the oven to 160°C (315°F/Gas 2–3). Lightly grease and line three baking trays with baking paper. Use an electric mixer or electric beaters to cream the butter and both the sugars together until pale. Beat in the eggs and vanilla until combined. Beat in the flour and salt, scraping down the side of the bowl occasionally, until just incorporated.

2. Add the choc chips and pistachios and briefly fold through with a spatula, then roll up your sleeves and use your hands to make sure the chocolate and nuts are evenly distributed. Eat the mixture off your fingers, then wash your hands.

3. Using slightly wet hands, roll heaped tablespoons of the mixture into balls and place on the trays, leaving room between each for spreading. Lightly press down on the balls to flatten. Bake for 18–22 minutes, depending on your oven and whether you like your biscuits chewy or crispy. Cool on the trays for 2 minutes before transferring to a wire rack to cool completely (but make sure to sneak in a few while they're still warm).

125 g (4½ oz) unsalted butter, softened

115 g (4 oz) white sugar

115 g (4 oz) soft brown sugar

2 eggs

1 teaspoon natural vanilla extract

260 g (9¼ oz/1¾ cups) self-raising flour, sifted

¼ teaspoon salt

200 g (7 oz/1¼ cups) white chocolate chips

100 g (3½ oz) pistachio nuts, halved

Warning: if you make these brownies, you're guaranteed to get lucky. There are no two ways about it. This recipe is not for the faint-hearted. Don't get me wrong, it's simple, but it's pretty darn rich. I tell people I only make them on special occasions, which is another way of saying any time I feel like brownies.

PEANUT BUTTER BROWNIES

PREPARATION TIME 20 MINUTES

COOKING TIME 30 MINUTES PLUS 30 MINUTES COOLING // MAKES 16 SQUARES

300 g (10½ oz/2 cups) plain (all-purpose) flour

240 g (8⅔ oz/1⅔ cups) salted peanuts, roughly chopped

150 g (5½ oz/1 cup) white chocolate melts

180 g (6⅓ oz) butter, chopped

250 g (9 oz) good-quality dark chocolate (70% cocoa solids), chopped

180 g (6⅓ oz/⅔ cup) smooth peanut butter

440 g (15½ oz/2 cups firmly packed) soft brown sugar

4 eggs, lightly beaten

1. Preheat the oven to 190°C (375°F/Gas 5). Grease and line a 24 cm (9½ inch) square cake tin with baking paper. Bring 1 litre (35 fl oz/4 cups) of water to a simmer over medium–high heat in a large saucepan, then reduce the heat to low.

2. Sift the flour and combine with the peanuts and white chocolate in a large bowl.

3. In a large heatproof bowl, combine the butter, dark chocolate and peanut butter. Put the bowl over the saucepan of simmering water. If the bowl is touching the water, just take some water out. Stir until melted and smooth, then add the sugar and stir until dissolved.

4. Remove the bowl from the pan, add the beaten egg and stir to combine. Fold in the flour mixture. Pour into the lined tin and bake for 30 minutes or until the brownie comes away from the sides, the top has cracked and the middle still has the slightest wobble when you shake the tin. Cool for 30 minutes, then turn out. Cut into 4 strips, then cut across the strips into 4 to make 16 squares. Pause to admire handiwork. Eat.

COOKING TIME WILL DEPEND
ON YOUR OVEN AND THE SIZE
AND SHAPE OF THE TIN YOU
USE. IT IS READY WHEN THE
OUTSIDE IS SET AND THE
MIDDLE HAS A SLIGHT WOBBLE
WHEN YOU MOVE THE TIN.

This is one of my favourite cakes in the world. I look forward to eating the left-over icing out of the bowl as much as the cake itself. There must be a million recipes out there for carrot cake, but this has to be one of the best.

AUNTY NET'S CARROT CAKE

PREPARATION TIME 25 MINUTES // COOKING TIME 65 MINUTES PLUS COOLING

SERVES 6

1. Preheat the oven to 190°C (375°F/Gas 5) fan-forced. Grease and line a 19 cm x 9 cm (7½ x 3½ inch) loaf (bar) tin with baking paper. Use an electric mixer or electric beaters to beat all the cake ingredients together for 2 minutes or until just combined. Transfer the cake mixture to the loaf tin.

2. Bake for 10 minutes or until the cake rises, then reduce the oven temperature to 160°C (315°F/Gas 2–3) fan-forced and continue baking for 55 minutes or until an inserted skewer comes out clean. Remove from the oven, cool in the tin for 10 minutes, then carefully remove from the tin onto a wire rack to cool completely.

3. For the cream cheese icing, use an electric mixer or electric beaters to beat all the icing ingredients, except the lime zest, for 3–5 minutes or until thoroughly combined, pale and creamy. Thickly smear the icing over the cake and scatter over the lime zest if it tickles your fancy.

150 g (5½ oz/1 cup) plain (all-purpose) flour, sifted
220 g (7¾ oz/1 cup) caster (superfine) sugar
1 teaspoon bicarbonate of soda (baking soda)
2 teaspoons ground cinnamon
½ teaspoon salt
2 eggs
60 g (2¼ oz/½ cup) chopped walnuts
125 ml (4 fl oz/½ cup) vegetable oil
235 g (8½ oz/1½ cups) grated carrot (about 2 small carrots)
juice of 2 limes

CREAM CHEESE ICING
60 g (2¼ oz/¼ cup) cream cheese, at room temperature
60 g (2¼ oz) margarine, at room temperature
125 g (4½ oz/1 cup) icing (confectioner's) sugar
1 teaspoon natural vanilla extract or vanilla bean paste
finely grated zest of 1 lime, to garnish (optional)

SALADS AND SIDES

It's hard to beat a good salad — so fresh, crisp and good for you. It's important the flavour is good too, and that the ingredients add some interest (not just the typical lettuce, tomato and cucumber combination I ate as a kid). Salads are a great example of the importance of texture in food; if you have a really soft ingredient (avocado, say) and eat it with something crunchy (walnuts) or something crisp (fried bacon), it becomes even more delicious.

I have also included my favourite side dishes — items to complement the main part of your meal and make it a little bit more special.

It's really important that you bring all your salad ingredients together with a dressing or vinaigrette; it unites the whole dish and helps the flavours of the ingredients shine. You can make dressings in big batches and in advance. They keep well in the fridge, but give them a good shake before using. It's important to only dress a salad just before you want to eat it or it will become soggy. Add the dressing, then carefully toss the ingredients with your fingers to coat everything. The followng dressings are really simple to make, and you can customise them to your own tastes. The general ratio is one part acid to two or three parts oil, depending on how sharp you like it.

SALAD DRESSINGS

PREPARATION TIME 5 MINUTES PER DRESSING // COOKING TIME NIL
EACH DRESSING MAKES ENOUGH FOR A SALAD TO SERVE 4 AS A SIDE

BASIC DRESSING
1 tablespoon white wine vinegar
1 teaspoon Dijon mustard
2 tablespoons extra virgin olive oil
pinch of salt

LEMON DRESSING
1 tablespoon lemon juice
2 tablespoons extra virgin olive oil
1 garlic clove, crushed
1 teaspoon Dijon mustard
pinch of salt

BALSAMIC DRESSING
1 tablespoon balsamic vinegar
2 tablespoons extra virgin olive oil
pinch of salt

JAPANESE DRESSING
1½ tablespoons rice wine vinegar
1 tablespoon light soy sauce
2 teaspoons mirin (sweet rice wine)

HONEY–YOGHURT DRESSING
95 g (3¼ oz/⅓ cup) Greek yoghurt
finely grated zest and juice of 1 lemon
2 teaspoons honey
pinch of salt and freshly ground black pepper

THAI DRESSING
1½ tablespoons fish sauce
2 tablespoons lime juice
2 teaspoons grated palm sugar (jaggery)

1. For all the dressings, whisk the ingredients together, or combine in a clean jar or container with a screw-top lid and shake vigorously.

QUINOA, POMEGRANATE & BROAD BEAN SALAD

PREPARATION TIME 15 MINUTES // COOKING TIME 15 MINUTES // SERVES 4

1. Combine the quinoa with 500 ml (17 fl oz/ 2 cups) of water in a saucepan over high heat and bring to the boil. Once boiling, cover and reduce the heat to a simmer and cook for 10–15 minutes or until all the water has been absorbed and you see a spiral pop out from the centre of each grain. Place some paper towel on a chopping board and spread out the quinoa to cool quickly and to absorb any excess water. Occasionally move around with a fork. Transfer to a salad bowl.
2. To remove the seeds from the pomegranate, lightly hit the whole pomegranate all over with a wooden spoon to loosen the seeds. Cut the pomegranate in half, position the cut side over a large bowl and hit again with the spoon to knock out the seeds. Pick out any seeds left in the halves. Discard any white bits that have fallen into the bowl.
3. Blanch the broad beans in a large saucepan of salted boiling water for 2½ minutes. Drain in a colander and rinse under cold water for 30 seconds or until cooled. Squeeze the beans to remove the outer layer of skin. Add to the quinoa along with the pumpkin seeds and toss together to combine.
4. Just before serving, pour the dressing over the salad and gently mix.

200 g (7 oz/1 cup) quinoa
1 pomegranate
370 g (13 oz/2 cups) podded fresh or frozen broad (fava) beans (from 750 g/1 lb 10 oz fresh in the pod)
40 g (1½ oz/¼ cup) pumpkin seeds (pepitas)
1 quantity honey–yoghurt dressing (see opposite)

ROCKET, PEAR & PARMESAN SALAD

PREPARATION TIME 10 MINUTES // COOKING TIME NIL // SERVES 4 AS A SIDE

1. Thinly slice the pear into thin wedges. Combine with the rocket, parmesan and hazelnuts.
2. Pour the lemon dressing over the salad and gently mix. Eat straight away.

1 ripe pear
60 g (2¼ oz) rocket (arugula) leaves (1 large handful)
80 g (2¾ oz) shaved parmesan cheese (shaved with a vegetable peeler)
40 g (1½ oz/¼ cup) hazelnuts, roughly chopped
1 quantity lemon dressing (see page 156)

I love the slight bitterness from the radish in this salad. It makes a great match with salty dishes, such as my teriyaki chicken (see page 51).

CUCUMBER & RADISH SALAD

PREPARATION TIME 10 MINUTES // COOKING TIME NIL // SERVES 4 AS A SIDE

1. Mix the vegetables in a large bowl.
2. Just before serving, pour the dressing over the salad and gently mix.

2 Lebanese (short) cucumbers, peeled, seeds removed and cut into matchsticks
4 spring onions (scallions), thinly sliced on an angle
4 radishes, thinly sliced
1 quantity Japanese dressing (see page 156)

This is a really simple salad that goes well with seafood or poultry dishes. Fennel has quite a strong aniseed taste, which is nice but big chunks of it can get a bit much, so take the time to slice it as thin as you can.

FENNEL, ORANGE & WALNUT SALAD

PREPARATION TIME 10 MINUTES // COOKING TIME NIL // SERVES 4

1 small fennel bulb
2 oranges, peeled and
    segmented
40 g (1½ oz/⅓ cup) walnuts
1 quantity basic dressing
    (see page 156)

1. To prepare the fennel, pull off any of the little dark green fronds and reserve for the salad. Trim the base by about 2 cm (¾ inch). Use a mandoline or really sharp knife to slice the fennel as thin as you can.
2. Combine the sliced fennel with the orange segments and walnuts in a bowl. Pour the dressing over the salad and gently mix, then top with the reserved fennel fronds.

This salad works really well with sweeter meat dishes (such as the super-quick chicken satay on page 48), but it can also be served as is for lunch, or even a light dinner with some noodles. Feel free to leave out the prawns if they aren't your thing.

THAI PRAWN SALAD

PREPARATION TIME 15 MINUTES // COOKING TIME 2 MINUTES // SERVES 2

1. Place the spring onion, mint, coriander, cabbage, peanuts, carrot and chilli in a large bowl and toss to combine.
2. Heat the oil in a large frying pan over high heat, add the prawns and cook for 1 minute each side or until just cooked through. Remove from the pan and set aside.
3. Pour the dressing over the salad and gently mix. Divide between bowls and top with the prawns.

1 spring onion (scallion), thinly sliced
½ cup mint leaves, torn
½ cup coriander (cilantro) leaves, torn
1 cup finely shredded Chinese cabbage (wombok)
70 g (2½ oz/½ cup) roasted unsalted peanuts
½ carrot, cut into matchsticks
1 long red chilli, finely chopped (seeds removed if you like it mild)
1 tablespoon vegetable oil
8 raw large prawns (shrimp), peeled and deveined with tails intact
1 quantity Thai dressing (see page 156)

This is a great little side to go with roasted meats and other hearty meals. If you can't find baby carrots, use two to three regular carrots cut into quarters lengthways, but keep in mind they may take slightly longer to cook. Try to get real maple syrup, not maple-flavoured syrup.

MAPLE-ROASTED CARROTS

PREPARATION TIME 10 MINUTES // COOKING TIME 25 MINUTES // SERVES 4

2 bunches baby carrots (about 20 small carrots)
2 teaspoons ground coriander
1 tablespoon olive oil
1½ tablespoons maple syrup

1. Preheat the oven to 200°C (400°F/Gas 6). Line a large baking tray with baking paper.
2. Trim the carrots, wash off any dirt and dry thoroughly. You can peel them if you want but you don't have to. Combine the carrots, ground coriander, oil and a big pinch of salt in a large bowl and toss to combine. Spread out evenly on the tray and roast for 25–30 minutes or until tender.
3. Use tongs to transfer the carrots back to the bowl. Drizzle maple syrup over and toss to combine. Serve immediately.

I never liked peas when I was younger, but when they're cooked with crispy bacon and some melted cheese, even a big pea-hater like me can find a reason to eat them.

CHEESY BACON PEAS

PREPARATION TIME 10 MINUTES // COOKING TIME 10 MINUTES // SERVES 4

1 teaspoon olive oil

2 bacon rashers, rind removed and sliced into 5 mm (¼ inch) thick strips

60 ml (2 fl oz/¼ cup) pouring (single) cream

70 g (2½ oz/½ cup) finely grated parmesan cheese, plus extra to serve

240 g (8⅔ oz oz/1⅔ cups) frozen peas

1 tablespoon lemon juice

1. Heat the oil in a heavy-based saucepan over high heat, add the bacon and cook, turning occasionally, until golden brown. Add the cream and parmesan and stir until the cheese has melted.

2. Add the peas and lemon juice and toss to combine. Stir until the peas are hot and just cooked through. This should take 1–2 minutes. Season to taste with salt and pepper, top with extra parmesan and serve immediately.

This is one of my go-to side dishes and it works well with most Asian mains. It's super quick and almost a meal in itself if you serve it with some rice or noodles.

SESAME GREENS WITH OYSTER SAUCE

PREPARATION TIME 10 MINUTES // COOKING TIME 5 MINUTES // SERVES 4

1. Heat a wok or large frying pan over high heat until hot. Add the oil, then the broccoli and bok choy and cook for 1 minute, tossing regularly.
2. Add the snow peas, stock and oyster sauce and continue tossing until the vegetables are just cooked (I like mine a little crunchy).
3. Add the sesame oil and toss to coat. Serve immediately, sprinkled with the sesame seeds.

1 tablespoon vegetable oil
350 g (12 oz) broccoli, cut into florets
3 heads baby bok choy, cut into quarters lengthways
150 g (5½ oz) snow peas (mangetout), trimmed
60 ml (2 fl oz/¼ cup) chicken stock or water
60 ml (2 fl oz/¼ cup) oyster sauce
1 teaspoon sesame oil
3 teaspoons toasted sesame seeds

Spuds are one of the most used vegetables in our everyday meals. The recipes on this page and the following pages are my versions of the classics.

SOME GOOD WAYS TO COOK POTATOES

ROAST POTATOES

PREPARATION TIME 15 MINUTES // COOKING TIME 1 HOUR 5 MINUTES //SERVES 4

800 g (1 lb 12 oz) potatoes
(about 4 medium)
½ teaspoon sea salt
2 tablespoons olive oil
6 thyme sprigs, leaves picked

> START THE POTATOES IN A POT OF WATER AND PAR-COOK THEM BEFORE THEY SEE THE OVEN. THIS MAKES THEM COOK MUCH FASTER AND, BECAUSE THE OUTSIDE SURFACE GETS ROUGHED UP A BIT, YOU END UP WITH A REALLY CRISPY EXTERIOR.

1. Preheat the oven to 200°C (400°F/Gas 6).
2. Peel and cut the potatoes into quarters. Place in a large saucepan and fill with enough cold salted water to cover. Don't start with hot water or the outside of the potato will be mushy while the inside will still be raw. Bring to a simmer and cook for 13 minutes or until a knife can be easily inserted into the potato. Drain in a colander and allow to steam for 2 minutes to dry.
3. Toss the potato around in the colander a little to rough up the outsides. Transfer to a large heavy-based roasting tray. Add the salt, oil and thyme leaves and toss around a bit so all the potato is coated. Ensure there is room around each potato so that they crisp up; if necessary, use two trays. Roast for 30 minutes, then take out of the oven and shake around to ensure even cooking. Return to the oven and roast for a further 20 minutes or until golden brown and crispy.

This is probably the most common side on many tables. It's a pretty darn versatile dish and goes well with just about any meat, poultry or fish you care to name. Use desiree potatoes if possible, as they produce a really fluffy and creamy result. To make your mashed potato a bit more special, add a spoonful of horseradish cream, or thinly slice half a bunch of spring onions (scallions) or chives and stir through at the end.

BASIC MASHED POTATO

PREPARATION TIME 20 MINUTES // COOKING TIME 20 MINUTES // SERVES 4

1 kg (2 lb 4 oz) desiree potatoes
100 ml (3½ fl oz) milk
100 g (3½ oz) butter

1. Peel the potatoes and cut into even-sized chunks. It doesn't matter if the shape is all higgledy-piggledy, but they need to be similar in size so that they take the same time to cook. Place in a large saucepan and fill with enough cold salted water to cover. Don't start with hot water or the outside of the potato will be mushy while the inside will still be raw. Bring to a simmer and cook for 13 minutes or until a knife can be easily inserted into the potato. Drain in a colander and allow to steam for 2 minutes to dry.

2. Now for the mashing bit. There are a couple of options here: you can either just chuck them back into the pan and squash them with a masher, or you can pass the potato through a potato ricer or push through a fine-mesh sieve with a spatula.

3. Once mashed, return the potato to a dry pan over low heat for 5 minutes, stirring occasionally with a wooden spoon to let the steam escape.

4. Heat the milk and butter in a small saucepan over medium heat until the milk is warm and the butter has melted. Add to the potato, fold to incorporate and season generously with salt.

There are lots of different ways to make homemade chips. Without being too modest, I like to consider myself a bit of a chip connoisseur. There was a period of time in my life where I had half a cow, potatoes and my good friend Adam Liaw at my disposal. We proceeded to make steak and chips seven nights in a row. I have found that deep-frying the chips twice, at two different temperatures, gives a delicious crisp outside and a fluffy inside. I use sebago potatoes (also called 'brushed potatoes'), but also look out for other varieties such as russet, King Edward and bintje.

CHIPS

PREPARATION TIME 15 MINUTES PLUS CHILLING // COOKING TIME 30 MINUTES // SERVES 4

1. Heat the oil in a deep-fryer, large saucepan or wok to 140°C (275°F). Peel the potatoes and cut into 1 cm (⅝ inch) wide chips. Add the chips, in batches, carefully to the oil and deep-fry for 5–8 minutes or until cooked through and starting to get a tinge of golden brown.

2. Use a metal slotted spoon or skimmer to remove the chips and place in a single layer on a tray lined with paper towel. Don't pile the chips on top of each other; use a second tray if necessary. Pat the excess oil from the chips with more paper towel. Transfer to the fridge for 1 hour or until chilled (see right).

3. Crank your oil up to 190°C (375°F). Add the chips, in small batches again, back to the oil and cook until golden brown. Remove from the oil, shaking the excess oil back into the deep-fryer and drain briefly on some fresh paper towel, leaving a bit of oil on the chips.

4. Transfer to a big bowl and season with salt while they are still nice and hot or the salt will all just fall off. Toss the chips around the bowl with the sort of enthusiasm one might have when running from a swarm of bees. Serve immediately.

1 kg (2 lb 4 oz) sebago potatoes
750 ml (26 fl oz/3 cups) vegetable oil, for deep-frying
sea salt

IF YOU HAVE TIME, PUTTING THE CHIPS IN THE FRIDGE BETWEEN THE FIRST AND SECOND FRYING HELPS TO DRY OUT THE OUTSIDE OF THE POTATO, SO THE EXTERIOR BECOMES NICE AND CRISPY.

Make sure you add the olive oil and lemon juice to the potatoes while they are still hot so the flavour soaks in more. I sometimes like to stir a big spoonful of grainy mustard into the mayonnaise before adding it to the salad.

CREAMY POTATO SALAD

PREPARATION TIME 20 MINUTES // COOKING TIME 20 MINUTES // SERVES 4

800 g (1 lb 12 oz) desiree potatoes (about 4 medium), peeled
2 tablespoons olive oil
1 tablespoon lemon juice
pinch of salt
60 g (2¼ oz/¼ cup) good-quality mayonnaise
3 bacon rashers, rind removed and cut into 5 mm (¼ inch) thick strips
2 spring onions (scallions), thinly sliced on an angle

1. Chop the potatoes into even-sized chunks. Place in a large saucepan and fill with enough cold salted water to cover. Don't start with hot water or the outside of the potato will be mushy and the inside will still be raw. Bring to a simmer and cook for 13 minutes or until a knife can be easily inserted into the potato. Drain in a colander and allow to steam for 2 minutes to dry.
2. While the potato is still hot, stir through the olive oil, lemon juice and a generous pinch of salt. Allow to cool, then stir through the mayonnaise.
3. Put the bacon in a non-stick frying pan over medium–high heat and cook until crispy. Transfer to a piece of paper towel and allow to cool.
4. Add the cooled bacon to the potato and mix through. Season to taste with salt and pepper and scatter over the spring onion to serve.

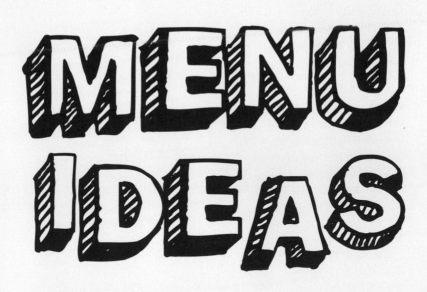

MENU IDEAS

Sometimes on special occasions one recipe isn't enough, so here are some suggestions for dishes that naturally go well together. Hopefully you will have as much fun preparing and enjoying them with mates as I have.

Try and make your life as stress-free as possible. Make as many components of the meal ahead of time. If you can, either make an entrée or dessert entirely in advance. Don't be afraid to recruit a helper. People love getting involved, plus it makes your job easier. Make sure you have plenty of drinks on hand; beer and wine are always good options. It's a good idea to look after your friends and have ample non-alcoholic drinks for anyone who can't drink or has to drive.

FIRST-EVER DINNER PARTY

MENU ONE
Spiced lamb with pomegranate couscous and honey–yoghurt
        dressing (see page 120)
Rocket, pear and parmesan salad (see page 159)
Blueberry frangipane with yoghurt granita (see page 130)

MENU TWO
Vietnamese prawn salad (see page 161)
Five-spice honey duck (see page 121)
Salt and pepper tofu (see page 53)
Cooked rice (see page 31)
Flourless orange and poppy seed cakes with cardamom yoghurt
        (see page 110)

MENU THREE
Crispy skin salmon with Thai salad and chilli caramel
        (see page 122)
No-set peach and raspberry cheesecake (see page 132)

The good news is that people love people who can cook, and so even a simple meal is sure to woo any potential dates. Actually, a simple dish cooked perfectly can be more impressive than a mediocre difficult dish. Your date doesn't want to lose you in the kitchen for hours — they want to see you! Make sure you check with your date in advance if there's anything he/she doesn't eat. There's nothing worse than spending an evening whipping up a fantastic pasta dish only to find out your date is gluten intolerant. Include desserts that can be made in advance and finished off after dinner to minimise your stress and maximise your date time.

COOKING FOR A DATE

MENU ONE
Individual chicken and mushroom pies (see pages 70–71)
Fennel, orange and walnut salad (see page 160)
Kyle's mum's gooey chocolate puddings (see page 79)

MENU TWO
Super-quick chicken satay (without the skewers) (see page 48)
Sesame greens with oyster sauce (see page 165)
Passionfruit, mango and blueberry Eton mess (see page 113)

MENU THREE
Mushroom and goat's cheese risotto (see page 119)
Rocket, pear and parmesan salad (see page 159)
No-bake chocolate cake (see page 126)

Occasions such as these call for dude food. Ideally, stuff that you can pick up and eat with your hands. Just make sure you have plenty of paper towel or napkins for people to wipe their hands with. Don't forget to have some cold beers in the fridge too.

HAVING MATES OVER TO WATCH THE FOOTY

MENU ONE
Skewered prawns with lime and sesame mayo (see page 89)
The ultimate cheeseburger (see page 144)

MENU TWO
It's burrito time! (see page 94–101)
Aunty Net's carrot cake (see page 153)

MENU THREE
Pulled pork buns with no-mayo slaw (see page 90)
Dude food corn (see page 147)
White chocolate and pistachio biscuits (see page 149)

The great thing about catering is that the food doesn't have to come out all at once. Make the desserts in advance, make the mayonnaise in advance, and have the pizzas rolled, topped, cooked and kept warm in the oven. Then they're ready for when your guests become hungry. Have some napkins or disposable plates handy too. It's a good idea to have lots of 'one-hand' food, so people can eat and hold their drink at the same time.

CATERING FOR A PARTY

MENU
Fiery sticky chicken wings (see page 86)
Skewered prawns with lime and sesame mayo (see page 89)
Pizzas (see pages 102–107)
Peanut butter brownies (see page 150)
Celebration cupcakes (see page 133)

These are some of the more challenging recipes in the book, but they are bound to impress. There are three distinct styles of menus here; the first is very meat 'n' three veg, so I would make this for my family. The second is a rather light menu that would be perfect for a summer occasion. The last menu is a bit heavier, but is good for a larger number of people because you can make the soup and tartlets ahead, and you can cook the pork the day prior, leaving you to basically just finish it off and assemble everything when your guests arrive.

COOKING TO IMPRESS

MENU ONE
Roast chicken with real gravy (see page 66)
Roast potatoes (see page 166)
Maple-roasted carrots (see page 162)
Cheesy bacon peas (see page 164)
Cookies 'n' cream ice cream (see page 82)

MENU TWO
Beef and pumpkin tagine (see page 78)
Cucumber and radish salad (see page 159)
Coconut panna cotta with mango, lychee and mint salad
     (see page 135)

MENU THREE
Confit pork belly with celeriac and apple slaw (see page 124)
Maple-roasted carrots (see page 162)
Passionfruit meringue tartlets (see page 109)

After a busy day, I just want food that I know I can start and finish preparing in less than half an hour. Something simple, but satisfying. I don't think 'quick' means that you need to sacrifice dessert either if you are a sweet tooth, so I have included some super-quick desserts.

MENU ONE
My favourite stir-fry (see page 47)
Fried bananas with salted caramel (see page 58)

MENU TWO
Teriyaki chicken (the proper way!) (see page 51)
Cucumber and radish salad (see page 159)

MENU THEEE
Chloe's favourite veal sandwich (see page 148)
Five-minute chocolate mousse (see page 57)

MENU FOUR
Salmon, lemon and caper fettuccine (see page 52)
Fennel, orange and walnut salad (see page 160)
Don't tell anyone there's an egg in it hot chocolate (see page 143)

INDEX

I feel incredibly privileged to have been given the opportunity to write
this book, and I could not have done so without the support, guidance and
knowledge of those around me.

THANKS!

To the amazing team at Murdoch who gave me the chance to realize my
dream of having my own cookbook (and in record time!), Amanda for giving
the book legs, Alice for coordinating everyone, Shannon for his ideas and
enthusiasm, Helen for the location and countless coffees, Kate and Lisa
for your help in the kitchen, Anneka for your pearls of wisdom, and Miriam
for her attention to detail.
To Bel and Nick, for their tireless work in editing.
To Hugh, for his work with feather and ink, and his constant Hughisms.
To Jess, for making the photography look awesome, and the chauffer service
in the silly car. To Kirsty, Mum, Dad, Gilly Bean, Gravy and Tess for shaping
me into the guy I am today.
To K-Mac, J-Bolt, Al-Meow, Willy-T and Skye, who give me inspiration, the
reason to include hangover recipes.
To the Masterchef contestants, judges and crew for an experience I'll never
forget, and for teaching me lots about food, and nothing about table tennis.
To Adam and Matt for giving me a roof over my head, and teaching me the
art of manliness.
To Lisa and Caitlin, for fighting my battles.
To all the chefs I have worked with for the invaluable skills and knowledge.
To Dan, for teaching me more about food than anyone.
Finally to Chloe, whom without her constant help, support and love I would
never have had this book.

Published in 2012 by Murdoch Books Pty Limited

Murdoch Books Australia
Pier 8/9
23 Hickson Road
Millers Point NSW 2000
Phone: +61 (0) 2 8220 2000
Fax: +61 (0) 2 8220 2558
www.murdochbooks.com.au
info@murdochbooks.com.au

Murdoch Books UK Limited
Erico House, 6th Floor
93–99 Upper Richmond Road
Putney, London SW15 2TG
Phone: +44 (0) 20 8785 5995
Fax: +44 (0) 20 8785 5985
www.murdochbooks.co.uk
info@murdochbooks.co.uk

For Corporate Orders & Custom Publishing contact Noel Hammond,
National Business Development Manager Murdoch Books Australia

Publisher: Amanda Maclean
Designer and illustrator: Hugh Ford
Editor: Belinda So
Food Editor: Nick Banbury
Photographer: Jessica Lindsay
Stylist: Miriam Steenhauer
Home Economists: Kim Meredith, Lisa McGill, Kate Wilson
Project Editor: Alice Grundy
Production: Alexandra Gonzalez

National Library of Australia Cataloguing-in-Publication Data
Author: Hann, Callum.
Title: The starter kitchen / Callum Hann.
ISBN: 978-1-742-667935 (hbk.)
Notes: Includes index.
Subjects: Cooking.
Dewey Number: 641.5
A catalogue record for this book is available from the British Library.

Printed by Hang Tai Printing Company Limited, China

IMPORTANT: Those who might be at risk from the effects of salmonella poisoning (the elderly,
pregnant women, young children and those suffering from immune deficiency diseases)
should consult their doctor with any concerns about eating raw eggs.

OVEN GUIDE: You may find cooking times vary depending on the oven you are using.
For fan-forced ovens, as a general rule, set the oven temperature to 20°C (35°F) lower
than indicated in the recipe.